THE FORGIVENESS OF SINS

The Forgiveness of Sins

MORRIS ASHCRAFT

BROADMAN PRESS / NASHVILLE, TENNESSEE

© Copyright 1972 · Broadman Press
All rights reserved
4281–13
ISBN: O–8054–8113–3

Library of Congress Catalog Card Number: 77–189500
Dewey Decimal Classification: 233.2
Printed in the United States of America

To My Father
HENRY H. ASHCRAFT

ACKNOWLEDGMENTS

A few years ago I taught a Bible study on "The Forgiveness of Sins" in the Baptist assembly of Glorieta, New Mexico. During that study, and in several church groups, members asked that I publish a study on forgiveness. The present volume is the result of that interest.

I wish to express appreciation to Mr. Bill Cannon of Broadman Press for encouraging me to prepare the study. I am grateful to several colleagues in Midwestern Seminary for discussing "forgiveness" with me. I express gratitude to two of my colleagues, Dean Roy L. Honeycutt and Professor B. A. Sizemore, for reading parts of the manuscript and for offering helpful suggestions. I acknowledge with appreciation Mr. Charles Calvert, minister of education in my church, who read the manuscript and offered suggestions for its improvement.

I gratefully acknowledge the assistance of my secretary, Mrs. Cheryl Dillingham, who typed notes and the first draft. I deeply appreciate Mrs. Nancy Calvert for typing the manuscript.

All Scripture quotations are from the Revised Standard Version.

CONTENTS

an attitude or appraisal unworthy of personal relationship; a working arrangement is merely a truce. Forgiveness is the restoration of a personal relationship; it is reconciliation.

"Forgiveness of sins" is a distinctively Christian term, and must be understood in its theological setting. At the same time, "forgiveness of sins" is a very personal experience and has very practical consequences. The term presupposes: God is personal Creator; God maintains a continuing interest in and relationship with men; man has sinned against God and is consequently alienated from him; God forgives men thereby restoring them to their original or intended relationship with him.

It would be helpful if we could maintain a distinction between "sin" and "sins," [1] but biblical terminology does not directly support such a distinction. The singular "sin" more accurately designates man's fundamental breach with God and its resultant estrangement. The plural "sins" are the specific acts of "sin," the bitter fruits which grow out of a heart that is evil (Matt. 15:19). Paul appears to prefer the distinction, although he uses the terms interchangeably in some instances (Rom. 7:8 ff.; 1 Cor. 15:3,17; Gal. 1:4). Sins are specific; they tend to become objectified. Sin and sins are personal. Personal man is responsible for sin.

Whether we speak of the "forgiveness of sin" or the "forgiveness of sins" (and both are biblical), we must maintain the biblical emphasis that sin is personal; its breach is interruption of personal relationship; its solution is restoration of personal fellowship. The use of "sins" appears to encourage the idea that sin is an object, or "something" with an existence apart from man.

There are two major interpretations of "forgiveness of sin": forgiveness removes the barrier of sin, and thus, prepares the way for reconciliation; and, forgiveness is the same as reconciliation.

The former view tends to see "sins" as separate and in need

of removal before the personal restoration can take place.[2] William Klassen holds to this view and speaks of forgiveness as "merely the prelude" to reconciliation.[3] It appears neater to speak of forgiveness, justification, reconciliation, and sanctification as if they were successive. There are several problems, however. Biblical terms often include part or all of the meaning of other terms. For instance, Paul used "justification" in preference to forgiveness, but intends to point to the same act of God's grace. Another problem is worded, "How could you call it forgiveness if it stops short of reconciliation?" Another weakness is that limiting forgiveness to the removal of a barrier encourages the idea that sin is an "object" separate from the man who did it.

The latter, and preferable, interpretation equates forgiveness with reconciliation. For instance, E. B. Redlich states forgiveness is "full restoration to fellowship." [4] The prodigal son may have moved successively through stages from want to awareness, repentance, confession and forgiveness, but his father paid no attention to a sequence. In one joyful act of forgiveness, he restored the boy to his intended place. This view of forgiveness preserves the personal emphasis. The penitent publican cried out in confession, "God, be merciful to me a sinner!" (Luke 18:13). The psalmist addresses God, "Against thee, thee only, have I sinned, . . . Wash me . . . cleanse me . . . purge me . . . fill me . . . create in me a clean heart, . . . Restore to me the joy of thy salvation (Ps. 51). Forgiveness is very personal; sin is not something separate from the sinner; forgiveness is the reconciliation of the sinner. It is not "merely a prelude" to anything.

The biblical writers used various terms to illuminate the theme of salvation. John used a biological term, "new birth," and Paul used a legal term, "adoption"; both terms point to the same event, God's "new creation" of man through Christ. Paul's legal term "justification" portrays God's acquittal of a sinful man, but he transforms the man in the process (Rom. 8:29). This term is very meaningful; Paul preferred it to "forgiveness" which he used sparingly. But both terms (and all of the other biblical terms) throw much needed light for understanding our salvation. Each makes its own contribution. Our task in this study is to understand the contribution of the term "forgiveness."

NOTES

1. Paul Tillich, *Systematic Theology III* (Chicago: The University of Chicago Press, 1951), p. 225 f.

2. Vincent Taylor, *Forgiveness and Reconciliation* (London: Macmillan and Company, Ltd., 1960), p. 25 f.

3. William Klassen, *The Forgiving Community* (Philadelphia: The Westminster Press, 1956), p. 212.

4. E. B. Redlich, *The Forgiveness of Sins* (Edinburgh: T & T Clark, 1937), p. 104.

II
FORGIVENESS IN THE OLD TESTAMENT

The early Hebrews understood their existence more in terms of the corporate life of the family, clan, or nation than in terms of individual life. It was not until the time of Jeremiah and Ezekiel that the individual with his responsibility for sin began to stand out in contrast to corporate responsibility. Consequently, the earlier ideas of forgiveness reflect the life of the community more than that of individual reconciliation.

Another factor of great importance in understanding forgiveness is that of the law. When the law states man's obligations to God, sin tends to be transgression of law, and forgiveness takes on a legal character. In this setting, sin brings consequences, such as suffering, defeat, and judgment, and forgiveness removes the consequences.

The sacrificial system, so foreign to modern man, was one approach to God in the Old Testament. In their offering to God, the Hebrews confessed their sin and sought God's forgiveness. Some Israelites may have believed that through sacrifice they were bargaining with God, but their instructions indicate a different kind of transaction. When bringing such offerings, the worshipers must "be accepted" by God, and their genuine repentance must be exhibited by their subsequent dealings with their neighbors with love and without grudge or vengeance (Lev. 19:5,18). The prophets certainly stressed the need for repentance, justice, and mercy or their sacrifices would be offensive to God. In the sacrificial context, forgiveness became the removal of the barrier of sin and the restoration of the people

15

to divine favor. In spite of the other factors, such as the legal
nature of corporate worship, the offerings must be brought by
those with penitent hearts [1] else God would not forgive.

Terms Meaning "to Forgive"

There are four main words in the Old Testament which mean
"to forgive." They are: (1) *salach,* "to send away"; (2) *nasa,* "to
lift up a burden"; (3) *kaphar,* "to cover"; and (4) *machah,* "to
blot out." Sin is the barrier between God and man, the object
which estranges. Forgiveness sends it away, lifts it up, covers
it, or blots it out.

Sending sin away. God may send sin away as one would
nullify a vow. For instance, a woman makes a vow to God which
proves to be contrary to the desires of her father or husband.
Even though vows are binding, in this case she may break the
vow and "the Lord will forgive her" (Num. 30:5,8,12). To forgive is to nullify the vow or remove the consequence which
would otherwise be imposed.

God may forgive sin in the sense of sending away its otherwise
inevitable consequences. Solomon, in his prayer of dedication,
prayed, "If they sin against thee—for there is no man who does
not sin—," and later repent, and pray to God, God will surely
forgive (1 Kings 8:46). A parallel passage presents the same
situation in a kind of forgiveness formula. If God's people (1)
"humble themselves," (2) "pray and seek my face," (3) "and
turn from their wicked ways," God promised, (4) "I will hear,"
(5) "and will forgive their sin," and (6) "heal their land" (2
Chron. 7:14). The same word appears in numerous passages [2]
and frequently deals with removing the consequences of sin.

Lifting up the burden of sin. Sin brings guilt which hangs on
the sinner like a curse, a plague, or a sentence of death. Forgiveness lifts the burden off. Joseph's brothers had sold him into
slavery out of sheer jealousy. Many years later, after their father
had died and they feared for their own lives, they pleaded with

Joseph, "Forgive . . . the transgression of your brothers" (Gen. 50:17). They begged for their dread to be lifted.

By the time the locust plague came upon Egypt, the Pharaoh had learned the word and its meaning. The plague enshrouded his land. He entreated Moses and Aaron, "I have sinned against the Lord your God, and against you. Now therefore, forgive my sin, . . . and entreat the Lord your God to remove this death from me" (Ex. 10:17). The king knew the plague was a curse, a consequence of his previous actions; he wanted it lifted.

When the Israelites sinned against God by making the idol of gold, Moses understood the seriousness of their sin. He sought forgiveness for the people in one of the most intense intercessory prayers on record. He confessed their sin in his prayer to God, and begged for forgiveness even asking that his own name be blotted out of God's book if God would not forgive them. (See Ex. 32:32.)

Several other passages teach this idea of forgiveness,[3] but none is as meaningful as Psalm 32. In the joy of his having been forgiven, the poet recalled the depth of his former misery while hiding his sin. When he had tried to conceal his sin, it burdened him down to the point of illness; his strength dried up; his body literally wasted away. But, when he acknowledged his sin to the Lord, the Lord lifted it away from him and restored his former joy.

Covering up sin. Sin is such that it leaves a stain which won't disappear; man cannot remove it. Like the blood of Abel, it cries out from the ground; it won't go away. Like a curse, it lingers to haunt its perpetrator. "Be sure your sin will find you out" (Num. 32:23). What can man do? Nothing! What can God do? He can cover it so that it no longer appears. When man becomes aware of his sin, he sees it as condemning evidence against him, but he cannot remove it. God graciously covers it; it no longer accuses man.

Jeremiah, in something of a nasty mood toward the enemies

who plotted against him, asked God not to forgive their iniquity
(Jer. 18:23). He wanted their ugly deeds to remain exposed so
that judgment would come upon them.

The figure of covering sin is related to the figure of God's
record book in which man's sins are listed. Although the particular Hebrew word is not used, the idea is that God forgives
man by destroying the list of his sins and no longer keeps a
record of his wrongdoing. "Blessed is the man to whom the
Lord imputes no iniquity, and in whose spirit there is no deceit"
(Ps. 32:2).

Blotting out sin. Sin leaves its mark as an indelible record, an
obvious consequence, or the brand of guilt upon the conscience.
There it is, and it demands judgment. When God forgives, he
just "blots it out." It is no more. Jeremiah used this expression
also in his pouting prayer against his enemies. He asked God
not to blot out the record of his enemies' sin (Jer. 18:23).[4]

God identified himself to his people as the one who "blots
out your transgressions" and promised not to remember them
any longer (Isa. 43:25). He claimed, "I have swept away your
transgressions like a cloud, and your sins like mist" (Isa. 44:22).
When God forgives sins, they just cease to be, like the morning
fog before the rising sun.

There is no clearer expression of this idea than in Psalm 51.
The psalmist, in deep agony because of his guilt, confessed his
sin, "I know my transgressions, and my sin is ever before me.
Against thee, thee only, have I sinned. . . ." Along with other
requests, such as "wash me," "cleanse me," and "purge me,"
he prayed to God to "blot out" his sins (Ps. 51:1-9).

God's power to blot out may be compared with his power
to create; indeed, it is creative power. In Genesis God spoke the
world into existence by his power. Prior to that act, only God
was. He created the world as out of nothing. That world (and
man within it) was good. But, when he sinned, man created a
deep contradiction in human life—a "thing" that curses him.

He cannot destroy it; only God can do so. God the Creator, who creates by his command, just blots it out, and it is no more. It was something, something awful; God forgives; now, it is nothing, nothing at all.

Witnesses to Forgiveness

Amos. In the last days of the Northern Kingdom, Israel, and in the shadows before night fell with the coming of the Assyrian armies, Amos from Tekoa proclaimed that God was judging Israel for her sins. He does not exaggerate the theme of forgiveness, but he cannot proclaim God's word of judgment without offering forgiveness even at that late date. God spoke through Amos to Israel, "Seek me and live" (Amos 5:4). In the vision of the locust plague, Amos prayed, "O Lord God, forgive, I beseech thee! How can Jacob stand?" God reconsidered and did not send the plague (Amos 7:2 f.). Forgiveness does mean the removal of consequences to Amos, but Amos also announced clearly that forgiveness was not available as divine response to sacrifice which was not accompanied by human justice and the repentant spirit.

Hosea. Having been sensitized through domestic tragedy and having learned the pain of loving and forgiving an unfaithful wife, Hosea understood God's attitude toward Israel. Along with the other prophets, Hosea knew the limitations of sacrifice (6:6) and the necessity for a penitent heart. He pleaded with Israel to "return" to God and promised that God would "heal" and "revive" his people (6:1 f.). In terms depicting tender family love, God spoke of his love for Israel, who like a child had often turned away from him but whom he had restored to the family and continued to love. This affection and restoration to fellowship after Israel's infidelity is a near approach to the forgiveness known in the New Testament (Hos. 11). His prophecy ends with the appeal, "Return, O Israel," and God will "take away" iniquity, and "heal" his people (Hos. 14:1–4).

Isaiah. Isaiah condemned Judah for being too concerned with the externals of religion while neglecting to correct the injustice and oppression among people (Isa. 1:2–17). He appealed to Judah to listen to reason, since awareness of sin may lead to repentance, and promised that if Judah turned to God, her sins which were as obvious as scarlet would be washed "as white as snow" (Isa. 1:18).

In the narration of his own call, Isaiah spoke of his own individual sin and the corporate sin of his people in which he shared. While Isaiah was in the Temple in worship, God appeared in a vision. In the presence of the Holy God, Isaiah saw his sins, as in a mirror, reflected from God's holiness. He confessed, "Woe is me! For I am lost; for I am a man of unclean lips." Such penitent response from man is followed by the forgiveness of God. One of the heavenly beings took a burning coal from the altar and symbolically purged the sin away from Isaiah's lips and said, "your guilt is taken away, and your sin forgiven" (Isa. 6:1–8). Forgiveness is purging or cleansing and removes or destroys, as by fire, the guilt of sin. Following this experience of forgiveness, Isaiah was ready to begin his prophetic ministry for God.

Micah. In the same vein, Micah called the people into court to defend themselves against the accusations of God. God was offended by their "thousands" of sacrificial rams and the "rivers" of oil offered in sacrifice, because the people had neglected justice, kindness, and the humble walk with God (Mic. 6:6–8). He closed his prophecy by reminding his readers that God is a forgiving God who, if men repent, will "have compassion," and "will tread our iniquities under foot, . . ." and will "cast all our sins into the depths of the sea" (Mic. 7:18,19). Forgiveness of sin removes sin and destroys it.

Jeremiah. Jeremiah's prophetic ministry extended through the long grim twilight before Judah fell to Babylon in the early sixth century B.C. His was the unpopular task of proclaiming to Judah that God's judgment was now coming to Jerusalem. Yet in the gathering gloom, he stood in the gate of the Lord's house and proclaimed God's word of promise, "Amend your ways and your doings, and I will let you dwell in this place" (Jer. 7:3). "It may be that the house of Judah will hear . . . turn from his evil way, and that I may forgive their iniquity and their sin" (Jer. 36:3).

By far the most important passage in Jeremiah on forgiveness is the promise of the new covenant. In that covenant, God's law will be inscribed on the hearts of his people; the relationship between God and men will be that of a family. God "will forgive their iniquity, and . . . will remember their sin no more" (Jer. 31:34). Sending sin away is the same as blotting it out. Forgiving sin is forgetting sin.

Along with Ezekiel (Ezek. 18:1–4), Jeremiah refuted the old saying, "The fathers have eaten sour grapes, and the children's teeth are set on edge." Both prophets saw that each individual man is responsible for his own sin (Jer. 31:29 f.). This becomes the context for forgiveness and, by the time of the New Testament era, forgiveness is an individual rather than a corporate matter.

Psalm 51. Psalm 51 does in the Old Testament what the story of the prodigal son does in the New; it says most of the essentials about forgiveness. In his plea for mercy (51:1–2), the psalmist approaches God on the right basis, God's "steadfast love." He has the correct understanding of forgiveness which is a blotting out of "transgressions," a washing from "iniquity," and a cleansing from "sin."

In his confession (51:3–5) of sin, the psalmist affirms several themes perceptively: I am the sinner and the sins are "my transgressions"; sin is an ever present fact as "my sin is ever before me"; sin is always against God. "Against thee, thee only, have I sinned"; God would be blameless if he did not forgive; and, sin is a part of my entire life, every part of it. The expression "in sin did my mother conceive me" is not a criticism of the mother but the acknowledgment of sin in the totality of life, even from its beginning.

The acknowledgment of God's expectation of man provides the proper motivation for repenting (51:6–8): God desires that man shall be true inwardly; therefore, only purging and cleansing by God can prepare man for living with God; the result is "joy and gladness," the true destiny of man.

The psalmist knew the nature of forgiveness (51:9–12): Sins must be removed by God's hiding his "face" or blotting out iniquities. Forgiveness is creative in that it creates a "clean heart," and a "right spirit" in man. Forgiveness is reconciliation with God as indicated in the plea, "Cast me not away from thy presence, and take not thy Holy Spirit from me." Forgiveness is a restoration characterized by joy.

Forgiveness brings about changes in man: now he vows (51: 13–15) to "teach transgressors" and to reclaim other "sinners." He pledges to "sing aloud" of God's "deliverance" and to praise God.

The psalmist acknowledges a new understanding of God (16–17) now that he is forgiven. God does not "delight in sacrifice"; God desires a "broken and contrite heart." The personal nature of reconciliation overshadows the legal and sacrificial aspects.

Summary

Only God can forgive sin, since sin is against God. The psalmist (51:4) said it most clearly. In the covenant relation, a man doing a wrong against his neighbor is actually sinning against God. God is the Creator; he gave the law; he created man. Failure to acknowledge God, violation of his law, and wrongdoing to another man is sin; it estranges from God.

The conditions for forgiveness are repentance and confession.[5] Repentance is the actual turning to God from sin; confession is the acknowledgment of the fact of sin, and its guilt, in the acceptance of forgiveness. In some cases men are exhorted to pray, amend their ways, do justly, and present broken and contrite hearts to God if they would be forgiven. These may also be conditions.

The immediate results of forgiveness, if not actually forgiveness, are restoration to God, lifting of guilt or suffering, cleansing, purging, healing, and restoration of strength and joy. These themes suggest reconciliation.

Forgiveness is the only solution for human sin; no alternative is suggested in the Old Testament. Forgiveness is a creative act. Israel must change her ways, pray, repent, and do justly; but, God forgives.

It is never too late to repent and receive God's forgiveness. The offer is extended by the prophets even as the judgment falls.

Forgiveness is forgetting sin. Jeremiah saw it correctly and stated, "I will forgive their iniquity, and I will remember their sin no more" (Jer. 31:34). When God forgives iniquity, the psalmist says, "as far as the east is from the west, so far does he remove our transgressions from us" (103:12). Other men may be less charitable to us; we may torture ourselves needlessly by recalling our sins; but, when God forgives sin, he forgets it as if it had never happened. He will never bring it up again!

NOTES

1. Henry Barclay Swete, *The Forgiveness of Sins* (Edinburgh: T & T Clark, 1937), p. 21.

2. Psalm 103:3; Jeremiah 31:31–34; Jeremiah 36:3; Daniel 9:19; Amos 7:2; Leviticus 4:20,26,31,35; 5:10,13,16,18; 6:7; 19:22; Numbers 15:25,26,28.

3. Numbers 14:19; Joshua 24:19; 1 Samuel 25:28; Psalms 25:18; 85:2; 99:8; 32:1; Isaiah 2:9; 33:24.

4. See also Nehemiah 4:5; Psalm 109:14.

5. See E. B. Redlich, *The Forgiveness of Sins* (Edinburgh: T & T Clark, 1937), for two chapters "The Pre-Prophetic Age," and "The Prophetic Age," and a "Summary" on the Old Testament teachings on "forgiveness," pp. 68–70.

III
FORGIVENESS IN THE NEW TESTAMENT

The Old Testament insights on forgiveness reappear in the New Testament, but there are some strikingly new ideas. The two most distinctive ideas are that Jesus "forgave sin" in his own name, and his followers proclaimed the "forgiveness of sins" in the name of Jesus. The former practice evoked the charge of blasphemy; the latter emphasis implies that in Jesus' life and death some new foundation was laid for the "forgiveness of sins." Jesus' teachings on the subject are radically new: he insisted that men could not have God's forgiveness unless they would forgive others. He required his disciples to forgive an offender as often as he repented, until seventy times seven times. He made forgiveness a completely free act of grace.

In the New Testament the legal element is beginning to disappear; forgiveness is primarily reconciliation of men to God and of men to men. There is still a preference for the plural "sins" in the formula, but the underlying thought is singular "sin." Sin is not so much an "object" requiring removal as it is a personal condition of estrangement from God requiring reconciliation. The conditions of forgiveness are still repentance and confession, but they are not acts which man can "do" as if to complete his part of the bargain. The whole act stands together as a single event. By the time of John the Baptist, who preached "a baptism of repentance for the forgiveness of sins" (Mark 1:4), forgiveness is practically synonymous with salvation. In fact, Zechariah had predicted of John that he would give knowledge of, "salvation to his people in the forgiveness of sins" (Luke 1:77).

The New Testament words are *aphiemi,* "to send away," and *charizomai,* "to be gracious to."

Jesus Forgave Sins in His Own Name

Only God forgave sin in the Old Testament. Jesus provoked the anger of the religious leaders, and drew the charge of blasphemy, by boldly declaring, "Your sins are forgiven."

The declaration: "Your sins are forgiven." Jesus was in a home in Capernaum. The crowd prevented four men from entering with a paralytic. They removed some shingles and lowered him through the roof into the room. Jesus said to the paralytic, "My son, your sins are forgiven" (Mark 2:5). The scribes charged Jesus with blasphemy because only God can forgive sin. Jesus responded in a statement which equated the formula, "Your sins are forgiven," with the statement, "Rise, take up your pallet and walk" (Mark 2:9), and then made the verbal claim regarding the authority of the Son of man to forgive sins.

While Jesus was dining with a Pharisee, a sinful woman entered the dining room, anointed Jesus' feet with ointment, wet them with her tears, and wiped them with her hair. Jesus declared to her, "Your sins are forgiven" (Luke 7:48). His parting word to her was, "Your faith has saved you; go in peace." Evidently, forgiveness of sin is the same as salvation. In the first case healing is also forgiveness; in the second case, forgiveness is salvation.

Jesus' defense: Authority of the Son of man. In Mark (2:10), Jesus claimed that he, as Son of man, had authority to forgive sins on earth. In the Lukan account, Jesus made the same claim and justification (Luke 5:24). Furthermore, Luke was quite certain that this was the mission of Jesus. He recorded that Jesus, early in his ministry, had interpreted Isaiah 61:1–2, which spoke of "release to the captives," as having been fulfilled that day in the presence of the people in the synagogue of Nazareth (Luke 4:21). He also reported that the risen Christ instructed his disci-

ples, "that repentance and forgiveness of sins should be
preached in his name to all nations" (Luke 24:47). These statements can only mean that Luke understood Jesus to be truly
Son of God and able to forgive sins. It is not clear how much
Jesus intended to convey about himself in this declaration, but
it was obviously intentional.

Jesus' Teaching on Forgiveness

Forgiving others is a condition of forgiveness. In the Model
Prayer, he related forgiving others to the acceptance of God's
forgiveness. Then, he explicitly reasoned, "For if you forgive
men their trespasses, your heavenly Father also will forgive you;
but if you do not forgive men their trespasses, neither will your
Father forgive your trespasses" (Matt. 6:14–15). The same
teaching appears in Luke (11:4). Mark related the same teaching
to prayer: "And whenever you stand praying, forgive, if you
have anything against any one; so that your Father also who
is in heaven may forgive you your trespasses" (Mark 11:25).

This emphasis is so distinctive that some scholars interpret
the whole Christian teaching of forgiveness on this basis.[1] It is
certain that Jesus did not intend a bargain between man and
God. Jesus was talking to disciples. They had already come to
know God's forgiveness; on this basis they could know how to
forgive others. It is likely that man's first acquaintance with
genuine forgiveness will come from God's forgiveness of his sin.
Then, he forgives others. This does not mean, however, that the
statement is weakened. Man needs God's forgiveness repeatedly, continuously. Jesus' teaching means just what it says.
Receiving forgiveness depends on forgiving others.

Jesus told the parable of the unmerciful servant (Matt. 18:
23–35) to establish this idea of forgiving as a condition of being
forgiven. The king called his servants to make an accounting
of resources entrusted to them. One servant, who owed 10,000
talents, could not pay. Upon his entreaty, the king "released him

and forgave him." In turn, this servant set upon his own servant who owed only 100 denarii and would not forgive him. The king called the unmerciful servant back, condemned him, and had him thrown into jail. Jesus concluded: "So also my heavenly Father will do to every one of you, if you do not forgive your brother from your heart" (Matt. 18:35).

Being forgiven requires more than just the mercy of God; man must accept forgiveness. Acceptance of free grace itself depends on one's ability to abandon pride and to acknowledge sin. Those who cannot feel this human frailty to the degree of forgiving others are simply unable to accept God's forgiveness. Repentance toward God is a basic change of mind and heart toward God, sin, and self. One who cannot forgive cannot be forgiven; he cannot accept forgiveness.

Forgive seventy times seven times. Jesus required of his followers that they forgive as often as offenders asked to be forgiven; he rejected all legalistic requirements and limitations on forgiveness. Apparently, there was a popular teaching that unusually pious people might be expected to forgive an offender as many as seven times, but this would surely exhaust both the patience and the capacity for forgiveness (Matt. 18:21; Luke 17:3). Jesus exploded this limit by requiring his followers to forgive "seven times in a day" (Luke 17:4) if the man repented.

Jesus' awareness of the offenses which separate people prompted him to give instructions to his disciples for settling disputes (Matt. 18:15–20). The offended brother takes the initiative and talks to the offender hoping to settle the problem. If he fails, he takes two others with him to arbitrate. If the offender refuses to listen, the matter is reported to the congregation. Even if all efforts fail, the only penalty is to regard the man as an outsider. Obviously, the point in each effort is to achieve forgiveness, reconciliation. This is evident in the question of Peter immediately after Jesus' statement. "Lord, how often shall my brother sin against me, and I forgive him? As many as seven times?" Jesus responded, "I do not say to you seven times, but seventy times seven" (Matt. 18:21–22). To the followers of Jesus, forgiveness is a way of life. They continue to receive God's forgiveness without limit; as occasions come they continue to forgive one another without limit.

Repentance is the condition of forgiveness. We have already noted that Christians were commanded to forgive an erring brother every time he repents (Matt. 18:21; Luke 17:3). Even if he sins seven times in a day, the only condition for forgiveness is his repentance.

This is very evident in the story of the unmerciful servant (Matt. 18:23–35). Repentance is a change of mind toward God with a resultant change toward men. This base fellow accepted pardon from his lord, but, in his abusive treatment of his own servant, showed that he was unrepentant and, hence, ineligible for forgiveness.

The clearest example is Jesus' story about the Pharisee and the tax collector. Both went up to the Temple to pray. The Pharisee stood in God's presence and boasted about himself and his religious achievements; the penitent tax collector stood hesitantly at a distance, beating his breast, and saying, "God, be merciful to me a sinner!" (Luke 18:13). Jesus announced that the tax collector went down justified simply because he had humbled himself. Repentance is a genuine change of mind toward God and sin. Justification and forgiveness are identical.

Forgiveness begets love, not license. It is often alleged that the free forgiveness of sin will likely encourage laxity and repetition of sin. It is obvious to one who has been through the pain of repentance and forgiveness that the person making such a charge has not made the pilgrimage. Jesus indicated that love and forgiveness are related. While he was in the home of Simon, the Pharisee, a sinful woman with a bad reputation entered and made a spectacle of herself in a lavish display of adoration for Jesus, even kissing his feet. The Pharisee reasoned that he was obviously no prophet or he would have detected what kind of woman this was. Jesus countered with the little story of the two debtors. One owed 500 denarii, the other 50. Both were completely forgiven by their creditor. Jesus inquired of the Pharisee which one would love him more. Simon grudgingly replied, "The one, I suppose, to whom he forgave more." Jesus commended his judgment in spite of his attitude, "You have judged rightly" (Luke 7:43). Jesus closed the incident by scolding the Pharisee's lack of courtesy so extravagantly corrected by the woman. He forgave the woman and cemented her excellence in love to the greatness of the forgiveness she had received.

Forgiveness is related to Christ's death. Jesus taught that he would be put to death and that his death would be related to his saving work. He predicted his death (Mark 8:31; 9:31; 10:33) and its relation to the salvation of men (Mark 10:45).[2] Nowhere is this more clearly stated than in the institution of the Lord's Supper. The Master said to the disciples, "this is my blood of the covenant, which is poured out for many for the forgiveness of sins" (Matt. 26:28). The early church proclaimed a message which always included some statement about Christ's death for the forgiveness of sins.[3] When Paul summarized the gospel tradition given to him and passed it on to the Corinthians, he rated "of first importance" that "Christ died for our sins" (1 Cor. 15:3). The exact answer to the question, How or why does forgiveness of sin hinge on Christ's death? has not been given, but every Christian must struggle with it.[4]

Forgiveness is reconciliation. Although many passages imply that forgiveness is really reconciliation, one passage teaches it superbly. The story is Jesus' parable of the prodigal son, or the "forgiving father" (Luke 15), even though the word "forgiveness" is not used. With a genius for brevity, Jesus told how the young man demanded his share of the family inheritance before he was entitled to it, how he went away and squandered his capital and disgraced the family name. Then, abandoned by his

fair-weather friends and desperate, he recalled the kind of man
his father was. He returned without money, and without a
reason for his behavior, he was armed only with genuine repentance and confession of sin. The father received him with honor
befitting royalty; he forgave him fully and restored him to full
membership in the family. He celebrated the occasion with his
friends. The joy of the reconciliation overshadowed the failure,
hurt, and loneliness so obvious in his previous departure. This
is forgiveness.

Jesus, with obvious intent to expose the hypocrisy of the
Pharisees and scribes, appended the story of the older brother
who was so set in his moralism and legalism that he had lost
the meaning of mercy. The grumbling older brother would have
locked the door against his younger brother, or at best, would
have admitted him in some probationary status. He knew no
thrill of love at the thought of another opportunity for making
a man out of a wayward boy. But, the father knew such emotional thrills; he had waited long for this occasion. God is like
this; he loves and forgives sinners; he forgives them and restores
them fully to his family.

Preaching Forgiveness in the Name of Jesus

We have noted that Jesus spoke of his forthcoming death and
related it to his achievement of man's forgiveness of sin. After
his resurrection, Jesus commissioned his disciples to preach
repentance and forgiveness "in his name" to all nations. In the
second volume of his history, Luke recorded how the early
church was faithful to this mission.

Peter's sermon, day of Pentecost (Acts 2:14–40). In the first
recorded sermon after the resurrection, Peter began by pointing
out to the crowd that God, according to his plan, had accomplished great wonders and signs through Jesus of Nazareth. He
charged some of the hearers with murdering Jesus but added
that God had raised him from the dead and made him Lord.

Some of the listeners were convicted by the message. Peter answered their question, "What shall we do?" with the challenge, "Repent, and be baptized every one of you in the name of Jesus Christ for the forgiveness of your sins; and you shall receive the gift of the Holy Spirit" (Acts 2:38).

Jesus' crucifixion was a crime; yet, God somehow worked through the event to achieve man's redemption. Repentance is a prerequisite to the "forgiveness of sins." The gift of the Holy Spirit either attends or follows forgiveness. The immediate consequence of forgiveness appears to have been acceptance into the Christian community—a genuine reconciliation.

Apostles' defense before the council (Acts 5:27–32). When opposition arose to the apostles' preaching, they were forbidden to preach. When they ignored the prohibition, they were brought before the council. Peter and the apostles summarized the gospel they preached: (1) "The God of our fathers raised Jesus whom you killed"; (2) "God exalted him at his right hand"; (3) "to give repentance to Israel and forgiveness of sins"; (4) "we are witnesses to these things"; (5) and "so is the Holy Spirit." The early Christian preachers understood this marvelous work of God in Christ to issue in the forgiveness of sins.

Peter's message to Cornelius (Acts 10:34–43). Luke traced the gospel from Jew to Gentile, from Jerusalem to Rome. In this incident, Peter preaches to a Roman centurion. The gospel story is the same to a Roman as to a Jew; the invitation is the same. "Every one who believes in him receives forgiveness of sins through his name."

Paul's sermon in Antioch (Acts 13:16–41). When Paul preached the gospel to the Gentiles, he narrated the same sequence of events and ended with the promise of forgiveness of sins in the name of Jesus Christ. In this narration, God's redemptive work reaches a climax in Jesus Christ; the resurrection of Jesus is of vital importance; the good news is that everyone who believes in Jesus receives the forgiveness of sins. In Paul's proclamation, forgiveness of sins includes liberation from the bondage which had prevailed under the law of Moses (Acts 13:39). It is quite significant that Paul stresses "believing" rather than "repenting." Neither is really possible without the other, but Paul's use of "faith" tends to include the other ideas.

Paul's defense before Agrippa (Acts 26:2–23). In his court defense, Paul narrated his own conversion experience and included a rather detailed statement of his mission. God had sent him to the Gentiles, "to open their eyes, that they may turn from darkness to light and from the power of Satan to God, that they may receive forgiveness of sins and a place among those who are sanctified by faith. . . ." Some very clear guidelines are obvious: (1) The mission of Christ, Paul, and the church is to bring forgiveness of sins to men. (2) This forgiveness of sins is based on God's work in Christ. (3) Forgiveness is granted after repentance, which is the opening of eyes and turning "from darkness to light and from the power of Satan to God." (4) Forgiveness of sins is a liberation, a release from bondage. (5) Forgiveness is reconciliation, a restoration to a "place among those who are sanctified by faith" in Christ.

In all of these passages in Acts, forgiveness of sins is the essential achievement of Christ and the point of preaching the gospel. It is reconciliation to God and to men. The priority of the forgiveness of sins is in evidence not only in these early biblical summaries (1 Cor. 15:3–8) but also in the earliest Christian formulas such as the Apostles' Creed.[5]

Continuing Forgiveness in the Christian Life

The forgiveness of sins, like repentance and faith, is not something one receives in conversion and then is done with. It is a necessary component of all Christian experiences.

Forgiveness for sins after conversion. The question about post-baptismal sins arose quite early. Every Christian is more sensitive to his sins after he has committed his life to Christ than he was before. He rejoices in his new relationship to God and the forgiveness of sins. But, his joy is interrupted often by the awareness that his victory is only partial, that he still is a sinner. What shall we do about our sins?

John, in the First Epistle, acknowledged both the fact and the seriousness of sins in Christians' lives, and correctly pointed to the only solution, repeated forgiveness. "If we confess our sins, he is faithful and just, and will forgive our sins and cleanse us from all unrighteousness" (1 John 1:9). It is the "blood of Jesus" which goes on cleansing us from our sins (1 John 1:7), since "Jesus Christ the righteous . . . is the expiation for our sins, and not for ours only but also for the sins of the whole world" (1 John 2:2).

Genuine Christians are never inclined to presume upon forgiveness and to continue sinning; John makes that clear. And yet, the most dedicated Christians do fall into sin; to deny this is to deceive oneself (1 John 1:8). We simply have to go back to the Lord day after day, seventy times seven times, in repentance, confessing, and asking for forgiveness. We must grow in the grace of the acceptance of forgiveness; this marks the victory over self-centered pride. This will never lead to a flippant attitude toward sin; repentance is too painful. The essence of the Christian life is that one is forgiven (1 John 2:12).

Christians forgiving others. Just as the Christian cannot endure without the repeated forgiveness of God, neither can he walk the Christian way without learning how to forgive others. The occasions for offense among Christians are numerous and grow out of normal human relationships. The ability to forgive and be forgiven quickly marks progress toward mature Christian life; the inability to do so arrests growth and makes for a stunted or distorted life.

The author of Ephesians knew the problem and the solution which faced the early Christians and it is applicable to us. He wrote, "Let all bitterness and wrath and anger and clamor and slander be put away from you, with all malice, and be kind to one another, tenderhearted, forgiving one another, as God in Christ forgave you" (Eph. 4:31–32; See also Col. 3:12–13). The word "to forgive" is *charizomai,* "to be gracious to." The high ethical standard herein prescribed forbids laxity in Christian living; but, even then, there will be sins for which the only cure is sheer forgiveness. The basis, or example, for Christian forgiving is that "God in Christ forgave" us. Christian forgiving is so essential that the church may accurately be described as "the community of forgiveness." [6]

Forgiving, a part of church discipline. A very important insight into forgiveness grows out of the troubled church of Corinth. There had been a problem so serious that it had affected Paul's plans to visit the church. The church had subjected the offender to a "punishment by the majority." Paul gives no hint as to what the offense was, but because he changed his plans about going there, one may assume that it affected him in some direct way. He also spoke of forgiving the person. The pain of the offense not only hurt Paul, but also the whole congregation. The punishment was evidently severe, but it was not exclusion.

Paul wrote to the church pleading for them, "to forgive and comfort him, or he may be overwhelmed by excessive sorrow" (2 Cor. 2:7), and "to reaffirm your love for him" (2 Cor. 2:7 f.). Then, Paul continued, "Any one whom you forgive, I also forgive. . . ." He stated that the overarching purpose was redemptive both for the offender and for the church (2 Cor. 2: 10 f.).

The passage encourages: (1) the practice of church discipline for an erring member; (2) quick forgiveness of the offender lest he be overcome by sorrow; (3) and forgiveness of the offender so as to redeem the congregation. It is quite obvious that even after punishment, whatever it was, forgiveness is the only solution—it is reconciliation. It is equally obvious that Paul, though personally offended, forgives along with the church of which he is a sharing member.

Radical forgiveness, blotting out the sin, is the Christian solution to the problems rising between and among persons. Even discipline, or punishment, aims only at bringing about the acceptance of forgiveness. Human groups usually punish with the idea of deterring wrongs, correcting the wrongdoers, or simply punishing the wrongdoer. Whether or not punishment deters crime is an open question; correction of the wrongdoer is a worthy motivation; retribution has no place at all in Christian thinking or practice.[7] The only "Christian" approach to the devastating estrangements among men is that of "forgiving" and seeking "forgiveness." This is what Paul meant when he wrote, "God was in Christ, reconciling the world to himself, . . . and entrusting to us the ministry of reconciliation" (2 Cor. 5:19).

Summary

In the New Testament, the "forgiveness of sins" is one of the most important ways of speaking of reconciliation. It is the same as justification by faith. Several teachings are distinctive. (1) Jesus forgave sin in his own name thereby assuming his role as Lord. (2) Jesus made forgiving others a condition of being forgiven. (3) He stressed genuine repentance as a condition of forgiveness. (4) The most distinctive element in the New Testament teaching on forgiveness is that forgiveness is offered to men through the saving act of God in Jesus Christ, or "in his name." (5) Practicing forgiveness in the Christian community is the very essence of its life. Christians can forgive because Christ has forgiven them. (6) Christians must forgive as often as the occasions arise; they can impose no limits. (7) The conditions of being forgiven are repentance, confession, and a forgiving spirit; the condition for forgiving another is merely his request. The Christian does not evaluate the offender's repentance, confession, or sincerity. (8) Forgiveness results in genuine reconciliation and love within the person forgiven.

Although the New Testament language, "forgiveness of sins," suggests its Old Testament background, and appears to favor an interpretation of "sins" as something objective to be removed, the New Testament understanding of "sin" is personal. It means the same to speak of the "forgiveness of sins" as it means to speak of the "forgiveness of sinners." This is of crucial importance in the discussion of the relationship between God's forgiveness of sin and the cross of Christ, as we shall see in the next chapter.

NOTES

1. E. B. Redlich, *The Forgiveness of Sins* (Edinburgh: T & T Clark, 1937), p. 139.

2. Vincent Taylor, *The Atonement in New Testament Teaching* (London: The Epworth Press, Third Edition 1958), p. 13 f.

3. C. H. Dodd, *The Apostolic Preaching and Its Developments* (London: Hodder & Stoughton, Ltd., 1951), p. 10 f.

4. *Infra,* Chapter IV, "Forgiveness And The Forgiver," subsection entitled, "God, The Cross, and The Forgiveness of Sin."

5. Henry Bettenson, *Documents of the Christian Church* (New York: Oxford University Press, 1947), p. 34.

6. *Infra,* Chapter VI, "Forgiveness and The Community of the Forgiven;" William Klassen, *The Forgiving Community* (Philadelphia: The Westminster Press, 1956).

7. C. F. D. Moule, "The Christian Understanding of Forgiveness," *Theology,* LXXI, (October, 1968), p. 437.

IV
FORGIVENESS AND THE FORGIVER

Two questions demand consideration before we proceed with the study of the Christian doctrine of the forgiveness of sin: What is the nature of God? and How is God's forgiveness of sin related to the cross of Christ? It is obvious that one's doctrine of God determines all other doctrines, but the question is particularly crucial with reference to forgiveness. The question about forgiveness and the cross is probably the most difficult theological problem raised in the entire study of forgiveness.

The Christian Understanding of God

All Christians do not hold to a distinctively "Christian" doctrine of God. Many sub-Christian and non-Christian views of God are prevalent among dedicated Christians. While an erroneous view of God does not necessarily bar one from fellowship with God, it certainly confuses all of his other beliefs and makes it impossible for him to state his beliefs correctly.

The "Christian" view of God is grounded in the event of Jesus Christ, historical revelation; it is not based on a general belief in deity. The first "Christian" statement about God is, "God is the Father of our Lord Jesus Christ!" Christians believe that God revealed himself most completely in the historical life of Jesus Christ. "God was in Christ." "The Word became flesh and dwelt among us." "For in him all the fullness of God was pleased to dwell, . . ." We may speak of God for a long time and never mention the Absolute, The Infinite, or the First Cause.

God who reveals himself. Christians, like the Hebrews before them, believe that the only God there is has revealed himself in history. They don't believe man can know God by meditation, good works, or prayer. God is known only when he chooses to reveal himself. God disclosed himself in historical events and inspired certain men to "hear" the word he spoke in those events. These men then proclaimed God's Word to his people.

Christians begin their doctrine of God with Jesus Christ, whom they consider God's fullest revelation, but they do not neglect the Old Testament. They understand the events of the Old Testament as God's revelation preparing men for the coming of Jesus Christ. A good example is the exodus from Egypt.

God called Moses and revealed himself to Moses; he gave Moses his name. Then, Moses was able to call upon God, maintain a relationship with him, and tell others about him. In the Exodus from Egypt, God revealed himself as the deliverer of the Hebrew people. Moses was inspired to "see" and "hear" what God was doing as he "acted" for Israel. Ever afterward, the Israelites spoke of God as their deliverer who led them out of Egypt. God is the God who acts for his people. The Old Testament contains numerous events of this nature.

God was in Christ. "But when the time had fully come, God sent forth his Son, born of woman, born under the law, to redeem . . . so that we might receive adoption as sons" (Gal. 4:4–5). The greatest revelatory event of all time was the Incarnation, "The Word became flesh and dwelt among us" (John 1:14), for in him, "all the fullness of God was pleased to dwell" (Col. 1:19). Even though Jesus was fully human—he hungered, thirsted, grieved, and died—he was preexistent with the Father (Phil. 2:5–11); and was the agent of creation (John 1:3; Col. 1:16). Indeed, Christians believe, "God was in Christ reconciling the world to himself" (2 Cor. 5:19). In Christ, men meet God.

This revelation of God happened historically in the person

and life of Jesus Christ. It was not a proclamation from "above," but a conviction from within evoked by the presence of Jesus Christ. Jesus did not overpower his hearers with irrefutable logic; he did not "wow" them with miracles. After he had taught the disciples for months, apparently without blurting out that he was the Son of God, he asked, "Who do men say that the Son of man is?" After the responses, he asked, "But who do you say that I am?" This is the midway mark in his ministry; had he not "told" them? Peter confessed for the group, "You are the Christ, the Son of the living God." Jesus blessed him and said, "For flesh and blood has not revealed this to you, but my Father who is in heaven" (Matt. 16:13–17). Apparently, God reveals himself in historical events and "inspires" men to perceive. Peter's confession was not an intellectual opinion; it did not grow out of curiosity or even interest; it was a conviction born of an experience with Almighty God through the historical encounter with Jesus Christ. In Jesus Christ, men meet God! They ever afterward speak of God as Father of the Lord Jesus Christ.

God is the Father of the Lord Jesus Christ. This confession indicates both how we claim to know God and what we believe he is like. The apostles were Hebrews and believed in monotheism; their belief in Jesus Christ as Son of God did not conflict with their belief that God is one.

In his life on earth, Jesus identified himself fully with man. He demonstrated what true man is like. He spoke reverently of God as Father, lived in this close relationship, and often prayed to the Father. His life indicates that man is to live as a child of God and is to maintain a relationship in which he addresses God as, "Our Father who art in heaven."

What is the Father like? In numerous ways and teachings Jesus revealed that God is the loving and forgiving heavenly Father who cares for his creatures infinitely more than an earthly father can. His parable of the forgiving father (Luke 15)

is one of the clearest presentations of Jesus' view of the nature
of God. God is the Father who loves and freely forgives a
wayward son. God is love. God's kind of love needs no motivation from the value of the object or person loved; God's love
is the unmotivated expression of his own nature. He does not
love because . . . ; he is love.

Jesus' view of God as Father does not neglect God's holiness.
God is other than man. In God's presence, man still stands in
awe. The disciples felt awe in the presence of Christ, and Christ
taught them in the Model Prayer to follow their address to God
as, "Our Father who art in heaven," with the recognition of his
holiness, "Hallowed be thy name" (Matt. 6:9–13).

Out of the prior conviction that God is the Father of the Lord
Jesus Christ grow other affirmations about God. He is personal.
One does not pray to an eternal principle or to an impersonal
deity who may have created the world but may have abandoned
it. The term "Father" demands that all conversation about God
be in personal terms in spite of some theological objections that
the term "person" imposes a limit on God's nature.[1] The personal nature of God as heavenly Father is clearly determinative
for the doctrine of the forgiveness of sin. Many of the errors in
understanding forgiveness grow out of the failure to recognize
the personal nature of God. For instance, when God is con-
ceived as judge in terms of law, there is no genuine forgiveness;
there is only leniency, pardon, probation, or mitigating circum-
stances. If God were an impersonal eternal principle, the word
"forgiveness" would be nonsense.

God's sovereignty is not minimized in the "Christian" view
of God. God is the Lord. Christ as agent of creation (John 1:3;
Col. 1:16) reveals God as Creator of the universe. Men without
faith can talk "about" God; men who know God by faith in
Christ speak of him as Lord and Creator. When they call him
"Lord," they acknowledge his sovereignty over their lives.
When they call him Creator, they do not speak of some theory

or explanation of the origin of things; they confess their faith that God is the source and, hence, the sustaining power and meaning in all that is.

Through Christ men learn not only that God is Spirit; they also learn through Christ what the Spirit of God is like. He is like Jesus Christ. The Christian statement of the triune nature of God is an attempt to state the "oneness" of God who is revealed by the Son as Father and Holy Spirit.

The Christian, and his theology, "risks" everything on the belief that "God was in Christ." Every other affirmation is grounded on this foundation. The Father of our Lord Jesus Christ is the forgiver of sin.

Popular misconceptions of God. Doctrines of God based on some foundation other than Jesus Christ, although begun on the basis of some worthwhile analogy, usually develop into sub-Christian or non-Christian views. Some illustrations will suffice and will show how crucial the view of God is for understanding the forgiveness of sin.

One of the so-called classic "proofs" for the existence of God begins with the observation of the orderliness of the universe. The teacher displays a timepiece, notes its precision and complexity, and asks, "Is it more reasonable to assume that this watch was designed by an intelligent being or that it just happened accidentally?" The answer is obvious. By equating order with "design" one argues that God is the *Great Architect* of the universe. This approach, if valid, would not establish what God is like—personal or impersonal, interested or indifferent—only that "he" or "it" is.

Numerous terms, chiefly from abstract philosophical reasoning, have been stated as pointing to qualities in the nature of deity. These qualities, such as spirituality, immutability, infinity, omniscience, omnipotence, omnipresence, immensity, etc., go on and on.[2] Albert Knudson spoke of these "attributes" as "something like pins stuck in a cushion." [3] The trouble with

the *Pin-Cushion View of God* is that one still does not have a
view of God when he decides how long the list is and how to
arrange it. Contemporary theologians prefer to speak about God
in terms of revelation rather than in terms of "attributes." [4]
Another misconception of the nature of God is found among
certain biblical theologians who subscribe to a view of inspiration which makes the entire Bible a horizontal plane with neither peaks nor valleys. They read through the Bible listing
God's characteristics on index cards. Then, using various
norms, they arrange the terms in some order and conclude what
God is. Of course, they have many correct insights into the
nature of God, but often resort to their own genius for arranging
the cards according to a priority of their choosing. For John
Calvin it was the idea of sovereignty. It is not likely that this
Index-Card View of God will be the same as the Christian doctrine of God. The Christian doctrine begins with Jesus Christ;
he is the norm which determines the understanding of and
arrangement of the other insights.

One example of the former error is the idea that God is the
Great Judge. The theme of judgment is clearly taught in both
Testaments; God is the judge. The problem is one of emphasis
or the starting point. If one begins with God as the *Great Judge,*
he will make religion a matter of law. Eventually, the law
becomes more authoritative than the judge who interprets it.
Jesus spoke often of judgment, but he opposed the understanding of religion as legalism. He spoke of God as Father. The
themes of love, holiness, forgiveness, and reconciliation along
with judgment fall into the proper relationships. Judges operate
within a prescribed area, the law. They may show mercy, com-
mute a sentence, or even pardon; judges take oaths to uphold
the law; they cannot "forgive." Forgiveness is not even pardon;
it is a new creation, a reconciliation. When God the forgiver
forgives, he blots out sin. This idea is likely to be lost if one starts
with the *Great Judge* idea.

Some misconceptions of God are drawn from a particular culture. The "Satisfaction Theory of the Atonement" is an illustration. It originated in the age of feudalism, when feudal lords fought duels and wars to avenge the slightest insult to their honor. Anselm of Canterbury thought of God as a *Feudal Lord* with absolute authority. In this concept, sin had offended God's honor, robbed him of his due respect, and satisfaction was demanded. The death of Christ was interpreted as a sacrifice to appease an offended jealous *Feudal Lord.* How different from Paul, who believed that God the Father was deeply involved in Christ's mission, and wrote, "God shows his love for us in that while we were yet sinners, Christ died for us" (Rom. 5:8).

Against the background of such misconceptions of God, the Christian understanding of God stands in bold contrast. God is the Father of the Lord Jesus Christ. God is the forgiver and reconciler.

God, the Cross, and the Forgiveness of Sin

The most distinctive idea about forgiveness of sin in the New Testament is that forgiveness is proclaimed "in the name" of Jesus Christ. This means the same as "he died for us" or "he died for our sins." Obviously, the point is that Jesus Christ has laid a new foundation for the forgiveness of sin. Our concern is with what this means. Stated in the simplest terms the question is, How is the forgiveness of sin related to the death of Christ? More often the question is stated, If God forgave sin before Jesus came and Jesus forgave sin in his lifetime and if he commanded men to forgive, was the cross necessary for forgiveness? An example of erroneous ideas of both God and atonement is seen in the wording, If God expects men to forgive one another without a sacrifice or payment for sin, why did he require the death of Christ on the cross as the basis of forgiveness?

To my knowledge, no one has offered a completely satisfac-

tory answer to the question. It would certainly be presumptuous
for me to think that I could even begin to deal with this question
in the limited space available, but we can go no further without
attempting to clarify the question and offer some suggestions
for its understanding. Numerous Christian scholars have devoted much of their time and talents to this question.[5]

Two factors which have contributed most to the confusion
are: (1) erroneous views of God; and (2) the tendency to objec-
tify, or depersonalize, the cross and sin. Consequently, two
guidelines are suggested: (1) Interpret forgiveness in the light
of the Christian view of God as revealed in Christ and avoid
all ideas which are inconsistent with it; and (2) speak of the cross
and sin only in terms of the persons and personal relationships
involved.

The cross is the cross of Christ. Since the crucifixion of Jesus,
the cross has stood like a mountain peak in history by which
men find their way. It is the one event, like the North Star,
which doesn't move or fluctuate. Men depend on it. But, it is
what it is because of who was crucified on it. It is the symbol
which holds together his life, its very nature, and his resurrection which followed. Apart from Jesus Christ who was there,
the cross would mark only the death of a hero or martyr. The
cross is the cross of Jesus Christ.

Upon the basis of abundant evidence in the life of Jesus, and
as recorded in the New Testament, Christians since Chalcedon
have spoken rather consistently of Jesus Christ as "truly God
and truly man."

If Christ was "truly God," as Son of God, and disclosed the
nature of God to us, we cannot think of a distant God demanding a sacrifice and the cross providing it. God in Christ was
present on the cross.

If Christ was "truly man," we must see his death as that of
a man. He came to disclose the nature of God to men, to seek
and save (reconcile) the lost. In the process, he incurred the

wrath of the religious leaders of the day whose teachings were threatened by his words and deeds. They plotted his murder; they lynched him. He did not go mechanically to the cross because God had placed the event on the calendar ages before; he went because sinful men, confronted by the disclosure of God, put him to death. These men were not unwitting servants of God; they were criminals. At any rate, Peter thought so (Acts 2:23).

Jesus Christ is the continuity which runs through the whole redemptive event. The cross is one chapter of that story; it would hardly be intelligible without his life before and his resurrection afterwards. The apostles did not isolate his death from life and resurrection but insisted on the continuity which the resurrection established (Acts 2:24; 5:31; 10:40; 13:37; Rom. 6:1–11; 1 Cor. 15:4).

The centrality of the cross is not threatened, but rather established, by insisting on the continuity of Christ through his life, death, and resurrection. The teaching about the cross has held a central position in Christian preaching, and this is proper. But, preachers should be careful not to remove the cross from its true context, lest they make an object out of it.

On the basis of God's revelation of himself in Jesus Christ, and a high Christology which insists that he was "truly God and truly man," we can consider what it means to say, "Christ died for us."

On the cross Christ died for us. There are two common phrases in the New Testament which point to Christ's death on behalf of sinners. The first is cast in very personal terms: Christ "died for us" (Rom. 5:8; 1 Thess. 5:10); "Christ died for the ungodly" (Rom. 5:6); he died "for all" (2 Cor. 5:14), for "everyone" (Heb. 2:9); and, we are to be patient with the weak brother "for whom Christ died" (1 Cor. 8:11). The second phrase is less personal: it is stated, "Christ died for our sins" (1 Cor. 15:3); and "Christ also died for sins once for all" (1 Pet. 3:18). These two affirmations are identical in meaning, but the latter one is more likely to be objectified and thereby distorted.

To say that "Christ died for us," must mean that he was in some definite way related to and involved with us. If a man is unconscious in a burning building and the fireman loses his own life in saving the man, one can say, "He died for the man." If a man is drowning in a raging current and another man saves him but dies in the process, it may be said that he died for the man. If, however, one deliberately dies in a burning building or plunges to his death in a raging current to show his love or heroism, he will be regarded as insane. Christ's death "for us" or "for our sins" is intelligible only in the light of the doctrine of the incarnation.

There are many pictures in the New Testament which were drawn in an attempt to show the meaning of the crucifixion. All of them are helpful; each one portrays an insight which complements the others; no one of them should be abandoned; no one of them should be allowed to eclipse the others. The work of Christ on the cross is like a beautiful diamond; it radiates beauty in all directions; each facet is but a part of the whole. One must look from different viewing points; it does not surrender its beauty to a single view.

In terms of Old Testament sacrifice, Jesus Christ was the Lamb of God whose sacrifice brings men to God (John 1:29; Heb. 9:11–12). He was the servant of Isaiah (Isa. 52:13 to 53:12) whose rejection, suffering, wounds, and stripes were really for us. He bore our iniquities. Jesus saw his suffering in terms of the servant (Mark 14:22 ff.). Christ's death, a crime of man, was also a redemptive act of God which condemned sin (Rom. 8:3). It was an expiation, or covering for sin (Rom. 3:25). When sin is seen as slavery, Christ's work is deliverance; he sets men free (John 8:34; 1 John 1:7; 2:2; 4:10). His death was like a ransom which sets the sinner free (Mark 10:45). The book of Revelation portrays Christ's death as a victorious battle with sin, death, and the devil. In the New Testament, Christ's death is understood as vicarious, sacrificial, and representative.[6] But, it cannot be stated in a single formula as the following theories of the atonement will indicate.

"The Ransom Theory," one of the earliest and most popular explanations of Christ's death for us, was based on Jesus' statement that his life was to be a "ransom for many" (Mark 10:45), and Paul's interpretation, "you were bought with a price" (1 Cor. 6:19 f.). The theory became popular in an age in which people lived under the constant threat of slavery. One could pay the ransom price for a slave and set him free. Christ did this for us. We were slaves of sin; Christ set us free. This view includes one very significant insight into Christ's atonement; it still has value. But, during its thousand years of popularity, it suffered much at the hands of prosaic churchmen. They added to its original meaning that God paid the ransom, Christ on the cross was the price, and the devil collected it. Obviously, such a view does an injustice to God and departs from the New Testament meaning of the cross.

The "Satisfaction Theory" of Anselm, published in *Cur Deus Homo?* was based on the idea that God is a feudal lord. Man's sin had robbed God of the honor due him. Two alternatives were open: satisfaction or punishment. Anselm chose satisfaction. Man had offended God; a satisfaction was demanded; man could not pay it, only Christ could do so. This view accurately sees the seriousness of sin and the holiness of God, but it overlooks God's role in Christ and the New Testament interpretations of Christ's work. It does a grave injustice to God, and makes the cross an external and legal transaction quite removed from the person who was crucified on it.

The "Moral Influence Theory" of Abelard, and "Example" theories in general, see Christ's death on the cross as an example which motivates man to repentance. God was always willing to forgive. These views have had great champions,[7] but they appear

to speak of only one side of Christ's work. They are not under-
girded by an adequate view of Christ.

The "Forensic Theory" [8] attempted to explain Christ's death
on the cross in terms of punishment (Anselm's other alternative). The theory was shaped in the age of absolute monarchies
and rising jurisprudence; the emphasis was on Law; god was
the supreme judge. Man was a criminal whose crime deserves
the death penalty; atonement is a legal device which allows God
to uphold his own justice and yet to pardon man. Christ ab-
sorbed the death penalty. The emphasis on punishment led to
the "substitutionary" views of atonement. In short, Christ died
"in our stead" rather than "on our behalf." If taken literally,
the view means that God vindicates his own justice by an act
which is unjust. No judge in the land would knowingly permit
one man to suffer the death penalty in the place of another. The
theory also overlooks the obvious fact that if a payment is made,
or an adequate punishment suffered, forgiveness would hardly
be needed.

Gustav Aulen, in his *Christus Victor,*[9] maintains that the New
Testament view (not a theory, which is too limited) is that Jesus
Christ engaged the powers of sin, death, and the devil in mortal
combat. The decisive battle was on the cross; Christ was victorious. This dualistic interpretation is not the account of a literal
battle; it is a great drama, hence his name "The Dramatic View"
(or "Classic View"). He thinks that the "Ransom Theory" is
but a degenerate form of the "Dramatic View." Aulen's view
enjoys considerable respect among other scholars and is a very
helpful work on atonement, but, of course, it does not completely deal with our question.

"Were you there when they crucified my Lord?" When we
keep the doctrine of the incarnation to the fore, and recall the
personal nature of salvation, we see ourselves also present in the
cross of Christ. He came to call us to God; he came in good
faith. But, like the servants in the parable of the householder,

we put him to death (Matt. 21:33–41). Like the spectators in Isaiah 53, we watched as he suffered rejection, wounds, stripes, and humiliation. After the fact, it began to dawn on us, as it did in the case of the Suffering Servant, that his suffering was for us. Then, and only then, do we see the cross as God's judgment on sin. It is not that God is collecting punishment from the only innocent person on the scene; rather, it is that I see myself as self-condemned in the shadow of Christ's cross.

Throughout the centuries Christian scholars have tried to spell out this "subjective" element in the atonement. This is what Abelard and Rashdall [10] were after. The old spiritual says it in the song, "Were you there when they crucified my Lord?" I was there; I was one of the mob which crucified him; I was also represented on the cross by perfect, obedient man. But, the cross is more than an example; we need more than an example or an inspiration. Our problem is not ignorance, but sin; we need help. The cross unleashes a power which saves men.

Paul clearly stated this theme, when he spoke of the death of Christ in such terms as: "one has died for all; therefore all have died" (2 Cor. 5:14); we have "died to sin" (Rom. 6:2,7); we have "died with Christ" (Rom. 6:8; Col. 2:20; 3:3; 2 Tim. 2:11). He believed that when a man comes to faith in Christ, the cross becomes a personal experience (existential experience) of crucifixion: "We know that our old self was crucified with him . . ."; and, "I have been crucified with Christ; it is no longer I who live, but Christ who lives in me . . . and gave himself for me" (Gal. 2:20). Vincent Taylor [11] calls this "representative."

Of course, this is somewhat subjective, but if one takes the incarnation seriously, sees the purpose of God in Christ, the responsibility of man for his own sin and for crucifying Jesus, the cross becomes the meeting point at which God meets man, man meets God, and man meets himself for the first time, and is redeemed.

Forgiveness in Christ's name is reconciliation. In biblical faith,
the "name" implies the entire person and work of the one who
wears the name.[12] The disciples cast out demons in Jesus' name
(Luke 10:17); they healed in his name (Acts 3:6); they proclaimed the gospel in his name (Acts 9:15). Consequently, when
they proclaimed the gospel of forgiveness ·in his name, they
proclaimed it on the basis of his entire person and work—not
just his death. To say "he died for us" or "he forgives our sins"
means the same thing; what Christ did reconciled us to God.
Our "sins" should never be thought of in some external way as
if separate from ourselves; neither should the cross be described
as separate from all of Christ's work which is personally related
to us throughout. If we recall the genuinely personal nature of
Christ's work and our experience of him, we are ready to speak
of the "cost" of our forgiveness.

Forgiveness is costly. The cross of Christ stands as an eternal
reminder that sin is serious and forgiveness is costly. But, one
will misunderstand the cross if he thinks of the "cost" as a price
demanded, or a commercial transaction of any sort.

When Paul wrote to the Corinthians, "you were bought with
a price," he certainly was thinking of the costliness of salvation;
it cost the life of Christ. It is the kind of cost one would mean
if he spoke of the love, suffering, and sacrifice called for in caring
for a sick or afflicted child. It is not a commercial thing; no one
demands a payment as some of the theories of the atonement
insist.

Whether we speak of the cost of forgiveness in terms of ransom, price, judgment, pain or suffering, or even penalty, the
meaning is the same. In no instance does God "inflict" it. Take
suffering, for instance. By itself, suffering is not redemptive;
some suffering embitters. Redemptive suffering is redemptive
because of the one who suffers, the reason for the suffering, and
the response to it; even then, the suffering is not the saving
agent; it merely attends the saving act. For instance, suffering

and pain attend the healing process of surgery and the recovery period, but suffering is not the healing agent. It attends the process. To be sure, Christ suffered for us and we suffer in the process of forgiveness, but no amount of inflicted suffering can produce forgiveness. It was Christ's giving himself to and for us in love. Theories based on a necessity for inflicted suffering miss the point of atonement.

The cross forever reminds us of Christ's life and death for us. It reminds us of our sin and its judgment. When someone asks, "Could not God have forgiven man in some less expensive way?" he misses the point. He has reverted to the commercial transaction error. The point is that, "God so loved that he gave. . . ." If one is forced to deal with the theoretical question, Could it have happened some other way? he can only answer, "Perhaps. But, it happened this way. I know of no other way."

The cost of forgiveness is very personal and painful in the confession, "I have sinned." Few things hurt more than the complete surrender of sinful pride and the acceptance of free forgiveness. The cross brings me to this confession. Even though it is followed by the joy of reconciliation, repentance and confession are painful experiences.

The cost of forgiveness is keenly understood by two long and dear friends who are alienated by a wrong. The more intense their respect for each other, the more they suffer in forgiveness. It is not that they are grudging in their forgiveness; rather, it is that each knows the pain he feels and then takes upon himself the pain of the other. Donald Baillie illustrated the suffering which accompanies forgiveness by the story of two such friends. Each knows his own pain, the pain of estrangement; each takes upon himself the shame of the other. Shallow friendships would not involve such suffering; such friends would hardly care. Forgiveness is not painful because it is grudgingly given; it is painful to admit wrong and to accept the wrong of another.[13] But, the suffering does not "buy" the forgiveness; suffering attends great forgiveness.

An estranged husband and wife are reconciled after being brought together by the serious injury of their child. His suffering did not, of itself, accomplish the reconciliation; it was not the "cause." Rather, it was the "occasion." Surrounding that event were two persons, and perhaps others, whose love, concern, and previous relationship contributed. The question is not, Could it have happened in some other way? The point is that in this event, each is moved to the awareness of love, mutual concern, and involvement by such factors as love, trustful commitment to each other, and the decision to start over. This is really what forgiveness is. It happened around the cross. In that event God so acted that he brought us back into his family.

NOTES

1. Paul Tillich, *Systematic Theology Vol. I* (Chicago: The University of Chicago Press, 1951), p. 244 f.

2. Augustus Hopkins Strong, *Systematic Theology* (Philadelphia: The Judson Press, 1907), p. 248.

3. Albert C. Knudson, *The Doctrine of God* (New York and Nashville: Abingdon Press, 1930), p. 206.

4. Emil Brunner, *The Christian Doctrine of God,* Dogmatics: Vol. 1 (Philadelphia: The Westminster Press, 1950), pp. 14–21; and "The Problem of the 'Divine Attributes' " pp. 241–247.

5. Robert William Dale, *The Atonement* (London: Congregational Union of England & Wales, 1909); James Denney, *The Death of Christ* (London: Tyndale Press, 1951); Peter Taylor Forsyth, *The Work of Christ* (London: Independent Press, Ltd., 1938); Hastings Rashdall, *The Idea of Atonement in Christian Theology* (London: Macmillan & Co., Ltd., 1919).

6. Vincent Taylor, *The Cross of Christ* (London: Macmillan & Co., Ltd., 1957), pp. 87–104.

7. Abelard Horace Bushnell, Hastings Rashdall.

8. Robert William Dale, *The Atonement* (London: Congregational Union of England & Wales, 1909), for an able presentation and defense of the Reformers' doctrine of atonement.

9. Gustaf Aulen, *Christus Victor* (New York: The Macmillan Company, 1951).

10. Hastings Rashdall, *The Idea of Atonement in Christian Theology* (London: Macmillan & Co., Ltd., 1919).

11. Vincent Taylor, *The Cross of Christ* (London: Macmillan & Co., Ltd., 1957), pp. 87 ff.

12. *"Onoma,"* ("Name"). *Theological Dictionary of the New Testament V,* Edited by Gerhard Friedrich; Geoffrey W. Bromiley, D. Litt., D.D., Translator (Wm. B. Eerdmans Publishing Company, Grand Rapids, Michigan, 1968), p. 272.

13. D. M. Baillie, *God Was in Christ* (New York: Charles Scribner's Sons, 1948), p. 173 f.

V
FORGIVENESS AND THE FORGIVEN

If the forgiver is God, the "forgiven" is man and his sin, or man the sinner. Although an underlying view of man is very obvious in the preceding chapters and will be more specific in subsequent chapters, a brief summary of man and his sin at this time will help in understanding forgiveness.

There are two major views of man in western culture: (1) the Graeco-Roman view of classical antiquity implied in Greek and Roman philosophy; and (2) the biblical view. Reinhold Niebuhr believed that all modern views of man are merely variations, modifications, or combinations of these two views.[1] The biblical view is more distinct against the background of the classical view.

Biblical View of Man

The classical view of man is rationalistic, dualistic, and optimistic. It is rationalistic in that it always sees man's rational faculties as his uniqueness; *reason* sets man off from things and other creatures. The dualism is usually expressed in a body-soul dichotomy; man's reason is somehow divine and dwells within his body; reason (or soul) is spiritual, divine, and good; body is material and evil. Such dualism led men to think that death was preferable to life, since it would liberate the soul from the evil body, a prison. The view is *optimistic* only in the sense that man's virtue is not stained by sin as it is in biblical thought. The classical view of man has no view of sin, only imperfection.

The biblical view of man is markedly different. Firstly, it

insists that man is always to be understood as *God's creature*.
This means, at least, that he is dependent on God, and is not
really man apart from God, and that in every sense of the word
he is a creature. His uniqueness is his "image of God"; his
creatureliness also stresses his finiteness. As a creature, finite in
all aspects, however, he is a unity rather than a dualistic being.
Secondly, man is a *sinner*. In his turning from God, he was
perverted into something less than true man. Thirdly, man is
capable of redemption. Sin did not completely destroy his original nature; he can still turn to God and be restored. This is what
forgiveness is about.

The image of God in man. The term appears seldom in the
Bible, but it stresses what man is. In both accounts of creation,
the writer tells that God made man in the "image of God" (Gen.
1:27), and in the "likeness" of God (Gen. 5:1). Men were forbidden to kill other men, "for God made man in his own image"
(Gen. 9:6). Although the word "image" does not appear in
Psalm 8, the uniqueness of man is clearly described in it in terms
of dominion over the rest of God's creation.

The "image of God" appears in three different ways in the
New Testament: [2] (1) it repeats the Old Testament idea of man's
uniqueness; (2) it designates the uniqueness of Jesus Christ; (3)
it points to the new nature of man when he is transformed by
faith in Christ.

Man's unique nature as "image of God" appears in the Epistle
of James (3:9) and in First Corinthians (11:7). Jesus alluded to
the same Old Testament idea when he requested a coin, and
asked, "Who's likeness and inscription has it?" When his critics
answered, "Caesar's," Jesus said to them, "Then render to Caesar the things that are Caesar's, and to God the things that are
God's" (Luke 20:24 f.). Evidently, the coin bore Caesar's image,
the man bore God's image.

Jesus' unique nature is the "image of the invisible God" (Col.
1:15; 2 Cor. 4:4) and "the very stamp of his nature" (Heb. 1:3;

cf. Phil. 2:5–11).

When man comes to Christ in faith, he "puts off the old nature," and is renewed after "the image of its creator" (Col. 3:9–10). By faith in Christ, sinful men are "changed into his likeness" (2 Cor. 3:18). When men are saved by faith, they are "conformed to the image of his Son" (Rom. 8:29).

Meaning of image of God. There is considerable disagreement among scholars as to the exact implications of "the image of God," but there are some agreements. "Image of God" in man designates man's uniqueness; it certainly does not mean that man is divine, or partly divine, because only God is divine in biblical thought. Whatever else the "image of God" may be, or may imply, it is certain that sin did not completely destroy it; man is redeemable.

What Is Sin?

I have tried to avoid objectifying sin even by discussing the subject separate from man, but some comments are appropriate. Then, we shall deal primarily with "man the sinner." Because of the availability of so many helpful discussions on the subject,[3] this summary can be brief.

In the Old Testament, sin is *missing the mark, transgression, rebellion, twistedness,* or *going astray.* All of the meanings suggest some wrong in man measured against some standard of God. Missing the mark suggests failure to measure up to the norm God expects; transgression is a violation of God's law; rebellion is a more willful turning against God; twistedness is the resultant depravity; going astray is departure from God with less rebellion and more indifference.

In the New Testament, sin is *unrighteousness, injustice, lawlessness, iniquity, ungodliness, impiety,* and *wickedness.* There are many other terms designating "sins." The sins are the acts of "sin." Sin itself is a state of the heart or man in his alienation from God.

Paul saw sin not as an individual act but as a state of humanity embracing not only the individual but also all of humanity. It was the rejection of God and the self-assertion of man both by men under the covenant and those who did not know the covenant (Rom. 1:21; 3:23). The law revealed the character of sin by holding up a standard. But the law, though good in itself, became the occasion for sin, which is a kind of demonic power, which rises up and destroys man (Rom. 7: 7–12). Sin, then, is the state of man before he comes to God by faith in Jesus Christ. Man's estrangement from God is so severe that man can actually be religious in his zeal for the law and unknowingly oppose God and persecute God's true people. Sin is a bondage.

W. T. Conner liked to portray the nature of sin as rebellion against God, unbelief, guilt, depravity, bondage, and an evil heart; sin results in alienation, degradation, disruption of the social order, suffering, and death.[4]

Sin as fall. In Genesis (chap. 3) there is a very informative account of man's sin against God. Although this term "fall of man" does not appear in the Bible, and the account itself has not shaped the biblical doctrine of sin as such, it states or implies very clearly what sin is. Man, who was made for fellowship with God, sinned. In his "fall" he was cast out of the garden, became a fugitive in a hostile world, and lived his days in suffering and toil. The account stresses man's intended purpose, the fact of his sin, the tragic consequences, and implies his redeemability.

To be sure, it is not an explanation of sin. An explanation would state in rational terms the "what" and "why" of sin; it would place the act in a cause-effect relationship. Sin is irrational; it is contradictory; it defies man's better judgment. No sinner can tell you "why." There is no rational explanation for an irrational act.[5] As we look into the account, however, several insights are clear. The tempter aroused distrust; sin is unbelief. The tempter suggested that by the act man could get "something

more;" sin is self-exaltation. Man reached beyond the limits of
creaturely existence and tried to grasp something that belonged
to God only; sin is rebellion. Sin is disobedience, and it results
in estrangement. Whatever the sin was, or whatever the "tap-
root" which sprouted all of these other sins, it was more serious
than casually eating fruit chosen from one among many trees,
which alone bore the sign, "Do Not Eat." Sin was something
which perverted the basic nature of man.

Sin as curse. Sinful life takes on an element of the accursed
(Gen. 3:14 ff.). This has nothing to do with black magic; it is
the result of man's wrongdoing. Man's sin disrupts God's creation, as well as man's inner being, and his social relationships.
Coleridge, in "The Rhyme of the Ancient Mariner," portrayed
a sailor who thoughtlessly killed an albatross and incurred hos-
tility of all creation. He and his comrades were subjected to
doom, a curse, and despair. The curse is the awful consequence
of sin. Sinful man must live in the awareness that he was created
for a better life; he struggles in a world he has turned against
himself. Albert Camus portrayed Jean-Baptiste Clamence in
The Fall as a man under a curse. Although Camus, and Clamence, did not believe in God, Camus saw clearly what the
"Fall" is and what its result is. Clamence was a successful
attorney who thought of himself as a champion of the widow,
the orphan, and the poor. One night as he walked across the
bridge, he heard cries from the river Seine below. A woman was
drowning; he could have saved her, but he turned and walked
away. The water was cold. This "fall" opened his eyes until he
saw every act of his life tinged with self-centeredness. He noticed
that after helping a blind lady across the street, he tipped his
hat to her after she had thanked him; she could not see it, of
course, but the bystanders could. His curse was to live in the
awareness that he was less than he pretended to be. Man in sin
lives under a curse of his own making.

Original sin. The psalmist wrote, "and in sin did my mother conceive me," (Ps. 51:5), and Paul wrote, "sin came into the world through one man. . . . Then as one man's trespass led to condemnation for all men, so one man's act of righteousness leads to acquittal and life for all men" (Rom. 5:12,18). These passages form the basis for the doctrine known as original sin. The doctrine actually stresses the universality of sin, and that all humanity is caught up in a web of sin.[6] The psalmist was not questioning the morality of his mother; Paul was not blaming Adam for his own sin. Paul said in the same statement, "because all men sinned" (Rom. 5:12). The psalmist was speaking about the fact that his entire life had been infected by sin. Paul was contrasting two ages: the age of Adam and the age of Christ.

The age of Adam was dominated by sin; we are all sinners in the family of Adam. But now that Christ has come, by his obedience and faithfulness to God, a new age has dawned. This is the age of Christ and justification. Paul did not mean to stress biological transmission of sin. If that were the case, he would have to be interpreted as saying that Christ's death results in universal salvation automatically. Neither in Adam's sin nor in Christ's faithfulness do men automatically inherit sin or salvation. Sin and faith involve personal choice in both instances.

Men have always sought for some way to avoid responsibility for their sin. The doctrine of original sin, when misinterpreted as biological transmission of sin, has been one of the most persistent pretenses. In biblical faith, man is never permittted to blame his sin on another. He must always confess, if he would walk with God, "I have sinned."

In Christian tradition, two terms have persisted in the interpretations of sin: pride and sensuality.

Sin as pride. Pride is man's self-assertion or exaltation against God. It takes various forms and guises. It appears to be an expression of his inordinate love for self. In self-centeredness, he forgets, ignores, or rebels against God. Then, he pretends that he is his own God. Paul seems to refer to such self-esteem when he spoke of natural man rejecting God because of his unusually high esteem for his own wisdom. (Rom. 1:21 f.). Reinhold Niebuhr says that such pride manifests itself in the pride of power, intellectual pride, and pride of virtue which is self-righteousness.[7]

Paul's conversion to Christian faith was attended by an awareness that much of his former righteousness had been a form of self-exaltation. He exalted himself even in his faithfulness to the law.

Man can detect this self-centeredness in all of his sins. He steals only because he exalts himself against God and over others. He kills, lies, commits adultery, and covets only because he thinks more of himself than of God or others.

Sin as sensuality. Sensuality is life according to pleasure and the senses. It is not necessarily immoral. Man comes to love the mutable goods of this world more than he loves God. In fact, despairing of God, he loses himself in worthwhile interests, such as family, work, or even religion. He finds his meaning in life in some area that is pleasant and rewarding. Back of this may be the inordinate love of self. Whereas, pride is the exaltation of self, sensuality is the losing of self in some of the temporary values of this world. This is the inauthentic existence as described by the existentialist theologians.

Man as Created

Although the following summary is not derived specifically from the term "image of God," it does stress what is unique about man; that is the intent of the term "image of God." In biblical faith man is: (1) a personal creature; (2) a creature in relationship; (3) a creature with freedom; (4) a creature with dominion; and (5) a responsible creature.

Personal creature. A person is a being conscious of itself as a self. A person can stand apart, as it were, and view himself as a self. He is able to exercise choice in the light of reflection. While other creatures may make primitive choices, and may be conscious, we have no reason to believe that they are endowed with the ability to engage in this personal reflection. We say God is personal, meaning that he has revealed himself to us as Father, and we know of no existence above the personal realm. God is not one of many in the category of persons, but God is personal. Man is in the image of God in that his existence is personal.

Creature in relationship. Man does not live alone. He was created in a special relationship to God, other men, and the world of nature. His relationship to God is one of dependence; it is expressed in obedience, trust, love, worship, prayer, and fellowship. In this relationship, man is always a creature of God, and consequently, always dependent on God. Man's relationship to other men is one of inter-dependence. Man has both an individual and corporate life and the corresponding obligations. Within the community of men, a man must live according to those laws which seek to preserve the life and rights of men. He must live in respect, love, care, and fellowship. He does not live apart. In fact, his relationship to God requires a relationship with men. His relationship to the world of nature is that of dominion. Man is to subdue the world, to have dominion over it. This means that he is sovereign under God. He must not only use the world, but he must care for it and preserve it. He is responsible for it. If man breaks with any of these relationships, he ceases to be fully human.

Creature with freedom. Man, in his true nature, is a creature with freedom. He is of such a nature that he can make choices on the basis of reflection. In such freedom he shapes not only his own destiny, but also, to an extent, that of his fellowmen. His freedom is limited but genuine. He has the fearful freedom of being able to say no to God. Those who advocate universal salvation imply, if they do not state it, that man cannot say no to God; he can only say, not yet. Eventually, his not yet must become yes. Biblical faith rejects this view, however it may be presented, not because of any limitation in God, but because of man's genuine freedom. Biblical faith insists that man has the freedom to say no to God, ultimately; that is what hell is about.

Creature with dominion. In Genesis (1:26 f.) and in Psalms (8), man is a creature who stands in relationship to the world as sovereign under God. His true nature is to reign, care for, preserve, and utilize nature. Like God, whose image he bears, he has a creative power to have dominion. God placed man in the world and told him to subdue it, and to rule it.

Creature with responsibility. Man's nature is that of a responsible person. H. Richard Niebuhr wrote a very helpful essay on "The Meaning of Responsibility." He, though writing in the context of ethical understanding, reflected the biblical view of man as a responsible creature. He maintained that the idea of responsibility includes four elements: *response;* action based on *"our interpretation"; accountability;* and *social solidarity.*[8] *Response* is man's ability and obligation to respond to God and to the situation of his own time; response is not blind obedience to law, but responding in the light of one's own understanding. *Accountability* stresses man's obligation to stand under the judgment of God and other men for his actions; he is answerable. *Social solidarity* stresses man's role in the continuing community of persons.

When we say man is responsible, we mean that he can respond to God and to his own situation; in fact, he is obliged to do so. To be responsible, he must reflect and interpret his life, obligations, and relationships and act accordingly; to obey legal demands blindly would hardly be responsible or "human." If man is accountable, he stands before God and answers for his life, accepting God's judgment and that of his fellows. He must give an account of himself; he is not outside the relationships of being under God, with men, and over nature. Man's responsibility for society is not limited to his own generation; he is responsible for doing right to his fellows and also to those yet to come. Although man's days may be limited to threescore years and ten, his responsibility, like God's, whose image he wears, goes on.

This is, in essence, what man is as creature of God. Now, we shall see what happened when man became a sinner.

Man as Sinner

In biblical faith, God always confronts sinful man with a call to repentance. From these calls and the information about man's life before and after his response, we learn what sin has really done to human existence.

Sinful man loses personhood. In turning away from the personal God with whom he has known fellowship, man loses the conviction that God, the Creator and Ruler of the world, is personal. This loss allows man to depersonalize himself, others, and human society. Even his religion becomes an impersonal system. For instance, in the days of Jesus, the religion of law had become very oppressive to persons. Jesus said of its leaders, "They bind heavy burdens, hard to bear, and lay them on men's shoulders; but they themselves will not move them with their finger" (Matt. 23:4). Law, as religion, depersonalizes God. For instance, it makes sabbath observance a chore; it was originally intended to guarantee persons a day of rest.

Man without God (the sinner) loses his own personhood. Persons are self-conscious and self-determining. They view their own selves, and make choices in the light of their reflection. The sinful man is possessed by a demonic master; he is a slave to sin. An inner compulsion becomes like a law in one's members, "I can will what is right, but I cannot do it. For I do not the good I want, but the evil I do not want is what I do" (Rom. 7:18 f.). Man so possessed that he is unable to choose freely in the light of his good judgment, and then do what he thinks is right, is less than a person.

Sinful man loses his regard for other persons; they become "things;" there is no greater offense to a person than to regard him as a "thing." The commandments forbid certain acts against persons; the sinful man commits those acts against them only when he has ceased to regard them as persons. When this depersonalization has reached full growth, things become more important than persons, or personal relationships. A rich young man came to Jesus seeking eternal life; Jesus told him to sell his possessions and give to the poor (This was not a customary requirement; this man's life was based on things, not persons.) and to follow. As he walked away he was very "sad"; his riches had won. When life is centered on things, the door to the Kingdom cannot be entered (Luke 18:18–30).

When sinful men lose their personal orientation, human groups become "collectives" instead of communities. Human collectives take on an existence of their own, but it is a demonic existence which always sacrifices persons for its own impersonal goals, as Reinhold Niebuhr has so clearly shown in his *Moral Man and Immoral Society*. What modern man can overlook the brutal force of the dehumanized collectives of men?

Sinful man is estranged. The first noticeable effect of sinning is estrangement from God; it is more correct to say that sinning *is* turning from God. Formerly, there was personal fellowship; now there is loneliness, flight, fear, and enmity toward God. Sinning is "going it alone."

Then, man is estranged from others. His community with other persons is broken. He can "sin" against them, exploit them, regard them as other than persons. He can even destroy them. His estrangement may be expressed in jealousy, envy, greed, lust, hatred, or death. Adam sins against God; Cain, his son, kills Abel his brother. Man's relationship to God determines his relationship with other men. Man's estrangement from other men has been clearly recognized in modern times;

life is characterized by its loneliness.

Man's estrangement within is the most horrifying of all. Paul's autobiographical statement of Romans 7 clearly portrays this anxiety of the self, "Wretched man that I am! Who will deliver me . . . ?" (Rom. 7:24). Only God can by forgiving man, thereby restoring him to the personal relationship with God, others, and self.

Sinful man is enslaved. Often, he proclaims his freedom very loudly, but man in sin has lost his freedom and is a bondservant of sin. Instead of exercising his freedom to be a person, to make choices in the light of his own honest reflection, he now bows to a demonic power. He is driven. Like the lion in a circus cage or Samson, blind and grinding at the mill, sinful man is on the leash of another. Although he was created in freedom, he has become a slave to his own sin (John 8:34; 1 John 3:8).

Sinful man is fallen. He was created to have dominion over the earth, but now the earth is a curse to him; it brings forth thorns and thistles, poison air, polluted water, and diseased land. Instead of reigning over it, he exploits it and wastes it, or idolizes it. Sinful man, having lost his relationship with God which determined his relationship to men and the world, approaches nature wrongly. Either he exploits it to ruin or worships it. Idolatry, worshiping the work of one's own hands, is forbidden, whether it be a statue of wood or a huge factory. Man's fallenness is very obvious in his relationship to the world.

Sinful man is irresponsible. Instead of responding to God and his human situation on the basis of his own rational understanding, he tries to live without responding or understanding. Instead of acknowledging his accountability to God and his fellowmen, he selfishly "goes it alone" to his own ruin and the hurt of all. He breaks the three mandatory relationships of man— with God, other men, and world—and tries to create a world of his own. He breaks with the society of which he is a part, ignores others today, and forgets about those yet to come. What greater lack of responsibility could there be?

Man the Forgiven

The whole story of redemption is concerned with telling how God restores sinful man. God forgives him; he reinstates him. Then, man again becomes a true person, in the right relationship with God, men, and world. He is freed from the bondage of his sin and again becomes responsible in his relationship to God, men, and the world. And this is the story of the forgiveness of sinners.

NOTES

1. Reinhold Niebuhr, *The Nature and Destiny of Man* (New York: Charles Scribner's Sons, 1949), p. 5.

2. David Cairns, *The Image of God in Man* (London: SCM Press, Ltd., 1953), p. 32.

3. See articles in Bible dictionaries. The articles on "Sin, Sinners," in *Interpreter's Dictionary of the Bible,* and *"Hamartano, Hamartema, Hamartia,"* in *The Theological Dictionary of the New Testament,* are especially thorough.

4. W. T. Conner, *The Gospel of Redemption* (Nashville: Broadman Press, 1945), pp. 1–49.

5. H. R. Mackintosh, *The Christian Experience of Forgiveness* (London: Nisbet and Company, Ltd., 1927), p. 61.

6. Conner, *op. cit.,* pp. 28–36.

7. Niebuhr, *op. cit.,* p. 186.

8. H. Richard Niebuhr, "The Meaning of Responsibility," in James M. Gustafson and James T. Laney (Eds.) *On Being Responsible* (New York, Evanston and London: Harper & Row Publishers, 1968). This essay was first published by H. Richard Niebuhr in *The Responsible Self* (New York: Harper & Row, 1963), pp. 47-68.

VI
FORGIVENESS IN INDIVIDUAL EXPERIENCE

God's act of forgiving sin may be regarded as a single event; man, however, appears to go through a series of stages in accepting the "forgiveness of sin." These are not necessarily sequential; they may be so intertwined as to appear as different strands of the same bond. At any rate, for the sake of clarity, some distinction is in order. In the acceptance of God's "forgiveness of sin," an individual comes to an awareness of God, a consciousness of his own sin, repentance, confession, and faith.

It is customary to speak of repentance and faith as the conditions of forgiveness. Certainly, they are on the way to forgiveness, or they are a part of the whole encounter. There is a problem in the word "condition." It must not be taken to mean that man does repentance and faith, and God does the forgiving. That sounds too much like a bargain. The experience is a personal reconciliation. Forgiveness of sin is from God's sides; repentance and faith are from man's side. But, God has something to do with calling forth both repentence and faith.

Acceptance of the Forgiveness of My Sin

The experience is very personal; it is *my* forgiveness. The word "acceptance" does not imply that there is a reservoir of forgiveness available for the taking; rather, it designates the inward, or psychological, personal decision which makes possible the reception of God's free act of grace. In other words, when I realize that I have sinned against God and cannot undo what I have done, in repentance, confession, and trust, I gratefully accept his gracious forgiveness. My acceptance indicates that I know that he has taken the initiative in bringing about my forgiveness.

If God is known only on the basis of his revelation of himself, it goes without saying that he has taken the initiative in my salvation. His initiative, however, is more specific: he sent his prophets; he sent the apostles; he sent his Son; he sent numerous witnesses with his word; he sends his Spirit. All of these join in calling me to repentance and forgiveness.

Experiences with God, as recorded in the Bible, often appear to have been quite sudden and without preparation, as if unrelated to a "past." In some cases, this may be so, but usually, God encounters us in relation to our preparation. Isaiah's encounter appears sudden, but he had gone to the Temple to worship and he knew quite a bit "about" God. Paul's experience on the road to Damascus sounds abrupt in the telling, but Paul knew all "about" God. He had interrogated the Christians; he had heard Stephen preach. God appears to us in such a way as to call us to "return" as if we had already known him. Perhaps, this is implied in the term "image of God" which all men bear. We belong to God; he calls us to "return."

The awareness of God. When I become aware of God, it is not only the awareness that God is but also that he is here, in this place. The ground becomes holy; I remove my shoes when I stand before God; I speak hesitantly about the depth of this awareness; perhaps, I never try to speak about the awe I felt in those moments in God's presence. God is Holy! His presence overwhelms me! In *The Idea of the Holy,*[1] Rudolf Otto used such terms as "Creature-Feeling," "Awefulness," "Overpowering-ness," and "Energy or Urgency" in an attempt to clarify this idea. In God's presence, I sense the depths of my creatureliness.

Moses was a fugitive from justice fleeing in the desert. God appeared in a burning bush and Moses was never again the same. Isaiah was in the Temple. He had been there before; so had God, but the two had not really "met." When he sensed God's presence, he fell in rapt worship and confession of sin; his life was never the same again. An arrogant young rabbi, Saul of Tarsus, knew so much "about" God that he could judge others' orthodoxy. On the way to Damascus, he "met" God. God asked the questions; Saul had no arguments. He merely said, "What shall I do, Lord?" Saul died that day; Paul, the apostle to the Gentiles was born.

The biblical writers spoke so dramatically about their encounters with God that most contemporary men conclude that God does not appear today as he did then. But, did not Moses, Isaiah, and Paul have an experience with God which is, for all practical purposes, the same as our own? They described the scenery as well as the drama, and we can't tell the difference. Moses' call is not about burning bushes; it is about God and Moses. Isaiah's call is not about the number of airfoils with which the seraphim were equipped in those days; it is about God and Isaiah. Paul's encounter is not about blindness at noonday, but the presence of God transforming his life.

God appears to us while we worship in church, meditate or pray at home, or when we go about our work. Sometimes, he speaks in his proclaimed Word. Sometimes, it is through the quiet spoken word of a friend; at other times, it is in the hearing of a hymn or song. But, in his own way and time, God appears to us. When I sense God's presence (usually in keeping with my own previous experience and knowledge), I am aware of what it means to be a personal creature in the presence of Personal Creator.

The awareness of God does more than make me aware of my sin; his presence motivates me to repentance. Jesus, as did John before him, preached: "The kingdom of God is at hand; repent, and believe in the gospel" (Mark 1:15). In plain language, he means that God is doing some great thing for his creatures, and we must not miss it. We must not miss the reason for our being.

The awareness of God brings us joy and hope. The prodigal son
was motivated to return as much by the memory of the kind
of father who waited as he was by the awareness of his own sin.
But, the awareness of God does bring an awareness of sin.

Consciousness of my sin. In God's presence, my sense of wonder is followed immediately by the sudden consciousness of my
moral uncleanness, my sin. For the first time, I see myself
reflected from the mirror of God's holiness. I join the prophet
in an exclamation of guilt: "Woe is me! For I am lost; for I am
a man of unclean lips, and I dwell in the midst of a people of
unclean lips; for my eyes have seen the King, the Lord of hosts!"
(Isa. 6:5).

The consciousness of sin is always *my* consciousness of *my*
sin. It has nothing in common with the theoretical statement
that "all men are sinners" even though the statement is true.
It has nothing to do with such statements as, "I know I am a
sinner, but I am as good as someone else." These appraisals,
whether true or false, are irrelevant. In God's presence Isaiah
confessed, "Woe is me! For I am lost." Peter, upon recognizing
that Jesus Christ was Son of God, cried out, "Depart from me,
for I am a sinful man, O Lord" (Luke 5:8). The penitent publican, before God's altar, pleads, "God, be merciful to me a
sinner!" (Luke 18:13). The prodigal son confesses, "Father, I
have sinned . . . ; I am no longer worthy . . ." (Luke 15:21).
In God's presence, you and I will also sense our own sin.

The consciousness of sin is my awareness of genuine guilt for
my sin. This has nothing to do with guilt complexes. This has
to do with the fact that I know that I have really sinned. I am
guilty. My hypocrisy has been stripped away by the presence
of God; I see myself as I truly am in the light of what I ought
to be. I don't like what I see. My feeble defense, "I try to treat
my neighbor rightly and live by the Golden Rule," suddenly
becomes an embarrassing lie. The fact is that I am a self-centered, greedy, and dishonest person. God made me for himself;

I have tried to live without him. My problem is not some non-sense about inheriting sin from my parents or being this way because of my upbringing or environment. My problem is, "I have sinned; I am guilty."

But there is hope even in this consciousness of sin. Does it not demonstrate that God's "image in man," though indistinct, still registers a claim on me. Is not this awareness an indication that man still responds to God who calls him to his destiny; forgiveness of sin opens the way.

The consciousness of sin is a healthy response, emotionally, mentally, and spiritually. It should not be confused with morbid internalizing. Paul distinguished between two kinds of sorrow for sin. One is a "godly grief" which produces repentance; the other is a "worldly grief" which produces death (2 Cor. 7:10). Some individuals appear to enjoy their remorse for past sins; they keep themselves and others reminded of it. This practice is not only "worldly grief" which will never lead to repentance and forgiveness, but it is also a very dangerous emotional risk. The genuine consciousness of my sin is an honest and healthy response: I acknowledge my guilt; I put the blame in the right place, and immediately move on to repentance and forgiveness.

The consciousness of sin, so necessary in receiving the forgiveness of sin, is also an evidence of human responsibility. Much has been said about man's being a responsible person under God and among his fellows. The acknowledgment of my sin is the most responsible action I can take. There are many subtle temptations, however, to blame someone else. I have mentioned the "misinterpretation" of original sin which insists on the biological transmission of sin. If that be true, I am not really responsible. The most outstanding temptation today appears to be that of blaming "society" for all evils.

Corporate responsibility for evil is acknowledged in the Old Testament; Christians know a community existence which requires of us that we accept the full responsibility of our corporate life. There is a tendency today, however, to forget personal individual responsibility and to blame society.

Several years ago in an American city, someone threw an explosive into a church building killing several black girls in Sunday School. The editor of a large city newspaper wrote an editorial in which he blamed all Americans for the crime. Although he was justifiably incensed at the heinous crime and at the social injustice which prevailed throughout the country, he failed to distinguish between two wrongs. He said, "We are all guilty"; but, while we may all be guilty of injustice, we were not all guilty for the crime being reported. When the late President Kennedy was assassinated, others repeated the same general verdict of "all guilty." The same cry was made at the murder of Martin Luther King. Recently, a man convicted by an appropriate military court for killing innocent civilians in the war zone denied individual responsibility and blamed all Americans for what he had done.

To be sure, men share a corporate responsibility for many evils which exist; however, most individuals would not commit the crimes mentioned. Nor would they condone them. When individuals commit crimes, they are responsible and guilty. Much more thinking needs to be done on our "corporate responsibility" for social justice. It seems appropriate to point out, however, that statements which make all men guilty in general, often tend to mean that no one is guilty in particular.

On the road to the forgiveness of sin, I acknowledge my sin. It is not someone else's fault; it is not the fault of society or environment. I am the sinner. This awareness prepares me to accept forgiveness.

Repentance. Repentance is turning to God. It is the kind of turning which grows out of a changed mind or attitude toward God. As such, it is positive; it is motivated by the awareness of God and the expectation of forgiveness. As a turning to God, it is also a turning from sin. Since God is the motivation and power for the turning, man could hardly turn from his sin unless he is first turning to God. Repentance may be the other side of faith, but in any event, they stand together. Paul described this event as, "repentance to God and of faith in our Lord Jesus Christ" (Acts 20:21).

Repentance stresses an inward change in man; it is like regeneration. Repentance is the decisive turning to God which grows out of the awareness of God and the consciousness of personal sin. This "change of mind" involves a changed attitude toward God, self, and other men.

The element of regret, or sorrow, in repentance has been exaggerated. In popular statements, "repentance is being sorry for one's sins," or "sorry enough to quit sinning." No amount of sorrow can produce repentance unless it is the "godly grief" which originates in the awareness of God's claim on my life and my failure to respond to him. Excessive sorrow may lead one to despair, even death; repentance may well include regret for sin, for lost years, and for harm done to others, but the sorrowful element is often overshadowed by the joy known in forgiveness. Repentance toward God is a change in man which prepares him for accepting God's forgiveness.

Confession. Confession is the acknowledgment of the consciousness of my sin to the person against whom I have sinned. Sin is against God; confession of sin is to God (Ps. 32:3,5). Sins are against God and other men; confession of sins is made to God or to the specific men against whom the sins were committed.

Confession is always in the first person singular, "I have sinned." A statement about someone else's sins is not a confession; it is either gossip or informing. The statement must be true, or it is not confession but perjury. The confession is the honest acknowledgment of my own sins. One could hardly "confess" his sins in general; confession is one's own acknowledgment, in the light of his own appraisal (which will certainly be shaped by knowledge of God) of his own situation.

Because of its vital role in Christian experience, the term "confession" has come to have a larger meaning. It designates the entire experience of accepting Christ; it is a confession of faith. "If you confess with your lips that Jesus is Lord and believe in your heart that God raised him from the dead, you will be saved. For man believes with his heart and so is justified, and he confesses with his lips and so is saved" (Rom. 10:9–10). Jesus' statement about "confessing" him before men indicated a man's decision to be identified with Christ.

Confession is made to the one offended; there is no demand for public confession of private sins. We should confess our sins to those sinned against, whether God or men. There is no reason for making such information public knowledge. Public declaration of sins would not be confession; it would be advertising. Now, if one has sinned against his family circle, he may well make his confession to that group (and a church is a family). But, a family would keep such information within the family circle as a means of hastening complete recovery and in order to minimize personal injury. Confession of sin and sins is an intensely personal matter. There is no reason for advertising the confession of sins.

Faith. This term tends to gather up the other terms in itself; it has become synonymous with the whole experience of knowing God. Specifically, faith is man's decision to commit himself to God in trustful obedience. One hears the call of God in the gospel; he believes that it is true; then, for himself he decides to trust his life to God. So, faith is a response to God. It "comes from what is heard . . . the preaching of Christ" (Rom. 10:17).

From man's side of the experience, faith brings the consummation of the forgiveness of sin. The personal transformation is complete, the relationships restored, freedom from sin accomplished, and responsible life of fellowship with God is begun.

Understanding Forgiveness of My Sin

God's forgiveness of sin is a creative act. The forgiven man "is a new creation; the old has passed away" (2 Cor. 5:17). As a "new creation," I have a new kind of existence. What does this mean?

In the previous chapter, we noted that God created man with certain characteristics: (1) Man is a personal creature who reflects his Creator's nature by being self-conscious and self-determining. (2) Man is a creature whose existence is set within a structure of relationships (with God, other men, and nature). (3) Man is a creature with freedom. (4) Man is the creature who has dominion over nature. (5) Man is a responsible creature who must respond to God, other men, and the continuing community of men in the light of his own interpretation and accountability.

We also noted how man's sinning disrupts his entire existence: (1) In sin, man loses his personhood, depersonalizes God and other men, and tends to depersonalize all relationships. (2) Estrangement from God, men, and self results when sinful man breaks his structure of relationships. (3) Sinful man is in bondage. (4) Fallen man, having lost his dominion over nature, either exploits it, loses himself in it, or idolizes it. (5) In sin, man is irresponsible in that he no longer responds appropriately to God or to the human community.

It is the contention of this study that in forgiving sin, God restores man to the intended image of God. God's work includes all that he has done for us of which Jesus Christ is always central.[2] A transformation takes place in man when he comes to the awareness of God, the consciousness of sin, repentance, confession, and faith. He is a new creation; he is forgiven, restored.

A new personal existence. The awareness of God as Personal Creator becomes the guiding force of forgiven man's life. The depersonalization of life and that of one's fellowmen gives way to the personal presence of God. This is the immediate result of the forgiveness of sin. In his Sermon on the day of Pentecost, Peter promised those who repent, "forgiveness of your sins; and you shall receive the gift of the Holy Spirit" (Acts 2:38). The personal presence of the Holy Spirit brings love into man's heart (Rom. 5:5); and, assurance, because the Spirit of Christ dwells within us (Rom. 8:9,12–17). The life of forgiven man is life "according to the Spirit" (Rom. 8:4) as opposed to life "according to the flesh." Rudolf Bultmann, following the theology of the New Testament in the language of Martin Heidegger, maintained that only personal, involved, decisive, and free human existence is authentic.[3] If man lives impersonally, it is inauthentic existence.

The intensely personal understanding of life brought about by God's forgiveness of sin sets the framework for all individual life and human relationships. Now, since I am a self-conscious person, living under personal God, I can be related to other men as persons.

Reconciliation to God and men. There can be no doubt but that sin is often treated as a barrier to be removed. But, this in no way detracts from the understanding of sin as personal turning from God and forgiveness as the reconciliation. Even if forgiveness of sin be understood as removing the barrier before reconciliation takes place, the whole act of forgiveness of sin ends with reconciliation.

In sin, men are estranged from God, other men, and themselves. Sin disrupted the entire relational structure of man's life. Man is a stranger fleeing from God; he is at odds with other men; the world of nature comes under a curse. God's forgiveness of sin restores the entire structure of man's relationship with God, men, and world. God becomes Creator, Lord, heavenly Father; other men are persons whom God created and for whom Christ died; the "world" is transformed into "creation," and as "creation," the "world" is good.

Modern man has sensed the loneliness of life without God. He has encountered the estrangements which shatter human existence into innumerable fragments. The ceaseless demands of self-centered individuals and human collectives have corrupted creation into chaos again. The frightful course of human history endows daily life with the dread of doom. The exploitation of nature threatens to make the "world" uninhabitable even before our generation is past. Men without faith cry out for reconciliation. Men who know the reconciliation of God in Christ through the forgiveness of sin are "ambassadors for Christ"; and have a "ministry of reconciliation."

Freedom from sin. God's free man became a slave to sin. The bondage was real. But, forgiven man says, "For freedom Christ has set us free . . . do not submit again to a yoke of slavery" (Gal. 5:1). Forgiveness of sin is a liberation from sin.

Forgiveness of sin is a victory over sins. Our basic sin against God resulted in sins against others. Forgiveness places man in a new relationship; he does not go on sinning as he did before. His victory is not yet complete, but he is progressively overcoming sins.

Man cannot be truly human unless he is free; a fully human life depends upon forgiveness.

Reconciled to the world. God's forgiveness of sin has a bearing on man's relationship to nature. We have noted that man was a kind of lord over nature, but in sin he lost that dominion. Restored man is right with the world. This is most obvious in his view of things; he is not a slave to wealth. Persons come first. He does not worship the work of his own hands; he worships God and rules over nature. Forgiveness removes the curse and changes "world" into creation. Man cannot keep his view of creation in perspective except when his view of Creator is in sharp focus.

Men without God exchange the "glory of the immortal God

for images resembling mortal man or birds or animals or rep-
tiles" (Rom. 1:23). Their complete alienation from God results
in estrangement from men and nature in that they dishonor:
"their bodies among themselves, and because they have exchanged the truth about God for a lie and worshiped and served
the creature rather than the Creator, . . ." (Rom. 1:24,25). But
now that God has accomplished justification for men through
Christ, creation itself shares in the victory. In some way, not
clearly understood, "For the creation waits with eager longing
for the revealing of the sons of God; for the creation was subjected to futility, . . . the creation itself will be set free from
its bondage to decay and obtain the glorious liberty of the
children of God. We know that the whole creation has been
groaning in travail together until now" (Rom. 8:19 ff.).

Renewal of responsibility. Man is a responsible creature; an
irresponsible man is less than human. Forgiveness restores what
sin wasted. Man stands again responding to God and to the
community of men. He accepts their judgment; accountability
is a cherished part of his responsibility. His reflection leads to
action. Only in this way can he be truly human.

Practical Implications of Forgiveness of Sin

Forgiving self. When God forgives sin, he endows man with
a keen sense of personal relationship to God. In the pilgrimage
to forgiveness, man passed through the experience of the awareness of God, consciousness of sin, repentance, confession, and
faith. Perhaps, we should assume that he has no lingering "problems with himself." Logically, it should follow that, if God
forgives me, everything is all right. Some scholars object to the
idea of man's forgiving himself, since only God forgives sin.[4]
But, men are commanded to forgive sins committed against
them.

It remains a fact that many people, whom God has forgiven,
go on with deep guilt in their lives. They struggle with the cruel

burden of past sins; they accuse and condemn themselves; they squeeze the joy out of life. If God forgives the sin and forgets it, why can't men forgive themselves? What right does a man have to ignore his frail creatureliness, and refuse to forgive himself even though God has. If it is wrong to "punish" another after forgiving him, is it not wrong to keep on "punishing" oneself after God has forgiven sin? The morbid tendency to hold one's sins against oneself is not responsibility; it is another way of asserting the sinful self against God, who forgives. It is an indirect way of holding on to self-centeredness.

Forgiving others. The nature of the personal experience of forgiveness leads to forgivingness. As forgiven persons, we are both inclined and able to forgive other persons. A spirit of forgivingness grows out of being forgiven. Living in forgiveness encourages the growth of the art of forgiving which endows life with a creative and redemptive principle. The forgiven man may have his greatest impact on the community of men by introducing forgiveness among men. "We are ambassadors for Christ."

Forgiving is the only hope. There is no other hope in many of the disrupted relationships among persons. A family was divided. A daughter had fallen into a serious immoral act; the family was catapulted into chaotic grief which disrupted every relationship within the home. They sought the counsel of their minister. The parents brought the charges and produced the evidence. The daughter defended herself, and added offensive statements about the parents' attitude. Later, she confessed: "I did it; I did wrong. I have admitted it. What else can I do?" The mother, after an additional outburst, lamented, "What can we do?" The minister replied: "There is only one thing you can do. I thought it had been obvious all the while. Your only choice is to forgive her." The hurt mother replied, "Forgive her? Just like that? How do we know she won't do it again?" The minister replied: "There is no way of knowing what she will do next week, but we can go beyond today only by forgiveness. She cannot undo what she has done. She has confessed her sin. What more do you want?"

Regrettably, the story has a note of resignation in it, and true forgiveness is not resignation; it is a joyful reconciliation. The parents should have been more willing to forgive, and more redemptive in doing so. By forgiving her, they could have helped her overcome her weakness; they could have restored joy and fellowship to the family; they could even have done something redemptive for their own personal lives.

In cases like this, and many of the personal disruptions in life, forgiveness is the only hope.

Forgiveness solves only the personal problem. Our personal difficulties often come to focus on "sins" as objects. Forgiveness restores the personal relationship; it may not solve the "problem" which precipitated the personal breach.

Two Christian men who lived on adjoining farms and had been close friends for years had a serious misunderstanding which began over a question about the property line between their farms. Harsh words intensified the feelings; both families became involved. Then, one of the men took the initiative; he went to his neighbor and apologized and asked for forgiveness. The other man also apologized, and they were reconciled; they forgave each other. The question about the property line remained. One suggested that they employ a surveyor, give him the deeds, build the fence along the line the surveyor indicated, and divide the cost of the survey. Forgiveness solves the personal problem; the surveyor solves the problem about the property line.

One misunderstands forgiveness completely if he thinks it will solve his problems with the Internal Revenue Service. It would be absurd for a man delinquent in payment of his taxes to ask the IRS representative to "forgive" him. There is no personal breach; this is not a concern for forgiveness. The taxpayer must just pay his taxes and whatever penalties are due. The IRS agent has an obligation to collect the taxes legally owed; he would be irresponsible if he "forgave" the debt.

The forgiveness of sin and sins endows the individual with a new lease on life, but it is not to remain an individual experience. The experience is of such a nature that it immediately involves him in a community of persons in which forgiveness is a way of life.

NOTES

1. Rudolf Otto, *The Idea of the Holy* (New York: Oxford University Press, 1958), pp. 8 ff.

2. Wilfred Knox, *Penitence and Forgiveness* (London: S.P.C.K., 1953), p. 1.

3. Rudolf Bultmann, *Theology of the New Testament, Vol. I* (New York: Charles Scribner's Sons, 1951), pp. 330 ff.

4. William Klassen, *The Forgiving Community* (Philadelphia: The Westminster Press, 1956), p. 213 f.

VII
FORGIVENESS AND THE COMMUNITY OF FORGIVING

The "forgiveness of sin" is so vitally related to the church in the New Testament that some scholars state that the theme has no meaning apart from the church.[1] We have noted: (1) Jesus interpreted his own mission in terms of forgiving sins (Luke 4:18). (2) He interpreted his blood in the Lord's Supper as given for the "forgiveness of sins" (Matt. 26:28). (3) He commissioned the disciples to preach the "forgiveness" of sins to all nations (Luke 24:47). (4) The early Christians so understood the mission of the church (Acts 26:18; 2 Cor. 5:19–21). (5) They proclaimed that message to the world (Acts 2:38; 5:31). (6) They understood the forgiveness of sin to be related to Christ's work and proclaimed it "in Jesus name" (Acts 10:43; 13:31). (7) Within the church they forgave one another (Eph. 4:32; Col. 3:13; 2 Cor. 2:5–11).

If the "forgiveness of sin" is related to the life and death of Jesus Christ, then his relationship to the church certainly requires that the study of forgiveness be related to the church.

In the previous chapter, we noted the individual's experience of forgiveness, how he comes to it, and what it means. We noted that forgiveness of sin restores the individual to God and to fellowship with other men. But, forgiveness is never merely individual.

Sin and its tragic consequences are rarely, if ever, limited to the lives of the two persons primarily involved; consequently, forgiveness of sin and sins extend to the other persons involved. For instance, the infidelity of a husband or wife injures at least

82

two families; their reconciliation will bless at least two families. This obvious, and inevitable, result in human relationships is but another expression of the fact that man is not only a creature of individuality but also of community. Outside the human community, he is less than human.

In the previous discussion of the nature of God, it was pointed out that the "starting point," Jesus Christ, is all-important. Starting from some other point inevitably leads into error. The same is true in understanding the church. If one starts by observing the institutions housed in lavish buildings scattered around modern cities, he may entirely miss what the church is. The starting point is Jesus Christ and the New Testament records. We are not concerned at this point with a survey of opinions expressed by disinterested bystanders about churches, whether those opinions be favorable or unfavorable.

The Church and the Churches

Origin. What we refer to as the church, and the churches, had its origin in Jesus Christ. Aside from the academic questions as to exactly "when" and did Jesus actually "found" the church, it remains that it is because he was. He called together a group of disciples and instructed them; he sent them on a mission; he gave them a message; he celebrated baptism and the Lord's Supper in that group. To be sure, his own resurrection completed the gospel message, and the coming of the Spirit on the day of Pentecost marked a significant date in the early days of the church. The people of God in the Old Testament are the spiritual ancestors, and we are the heirs. But, the church, and hence the churches, owes its distinctive existence to Jesus Christ.

The churches. Wherever the Christians went, they told about Jesus Christ; they proclaimed his gospel which was a call to repentance for the forgiveness of sin. This word of God was directed by the Holy Spirit; hearers were convicted; in their awareness of God, consciousness of sin, and repentance, they confessed and believed. As forgiven men and women, they were drawn together (this is what reconciliation means) into communities in which they worshiped, witnessed, cared for one another, forgave one another, and introduced this gospel of forgiveness to others outside the community. These enlarged communities of forgiven sinners were churches. They sprang up wherever the gospel was preached. The church and the churches are mentioned in the New Testament about 114 times, of which about 93 refer to such local congregations, churches.

The men and women of these communities shared a common experience and life with those of other church communities. They came to see the unity in Christian faith—we are all one family in Christ. Paul stated this most clearly in Colossians and Ephesians, but the idea is found elsewhere (1 Cor. 12:27 f.). The church includes all Christian men and women of all ages. It transcends national boundaries, language barriers, cultural distinctions, and ecclesiastical organizations.

The church. There is quite a variety of terms in the New Testament describing the church, but the following distinctions are quite helpful.

The church is the *"people of God"* (1 Pet. 2:9 f.). This term fulfils the old covenant; the people of God are a people of a new covenant (Heb. 8:10; Rev. 21:3). The church, as people of God, is the new Israel (Rom. 9:6; 1 Cor. 10:18; Gal. 6:16; cf. Gal. 3:29; Phil. 3:3). The church, as people of God, is compared to a temple, or building (1 Pet. 2:4–10; 1 Cor. 3:10–17; Eph. 2: 11–22). The New Testament writers saw the followers of Jesus Christ as truly the people of the new covenant, the true Israel, and the people of God. Now, the boundaries had been broken; there was no distinction between Jew and Gentile, bond or free. The church is a new race of God's people. Its unity is portrayed in Ephesians (4:1–16).

The church is also the *body of Christ.* The human body with its diversity of members, each with a different function, united in a single organism and acting under a single head is a perfect analogy for the church (Col. 1:18,24; Eph. 1:23; 3:6; 4:12; 5:23). When Paul wrote the Corinthians (1:27 f.) about the "body of Christ" and its diversity of ministry, he spoke not of the church's locality but of its universality. This figure is supplemented by other figures, such as the vine and the branches. The term "body of Christ" always stresses that Christ is the head of the church (Col. 2:10; Eph. 1:22 f.; 5:23); that the church is one (Eph. 1:22; 4:4); and that the church depends on and receives its life from Christ.

The church is the *community of the Holy Spirit*. Jesus promised that the Holy Spirit would come and would continue to teach the disciples. The unusual coming of the Spirit on the day of Pentecost set the church on its way. At every juncture in the development of the church in the book of Acts, the church acknowledged its dependence on the Holy Spirit for guidance and power. The Spirit is one (1 Cor. 12:13) who gives unity to the church (Eph. 4:2). His gifts sustain the church (1 Cor. 12:4,8,9). Christian life is life "according to the Spirit," and we know the Spirit through Christ (Rom. 8:9). The Spirit is so much the life of the church, that one might correctly say that no community can claim to be a church unless it is formed by, unless it is led by, and unless it is sustained by the Spirit.

A church. A church is a particular manifestation of the church. As such, it is the people of God, the body of Christ, and the community of the Holy Spirit in this place. It stands in the historical experience of the people of God; it participates in the life of Christ's body; it is a community in which the Holy Spirit leads human life. If it is not so, no amount of structuring will make a church out of it.

There are other terms which express the genius of the church. For instance, the church may be called the "community of the Word." The Word was incarnate, then it was proclaimed, then

it was recorded. Men and women hear the Word and are called
to God. They are called together into a community in which
they both hear and proclaim the Word. This is what the church,
or a church, is. The church may also be called the "community
of forgiveness."

The Church—A Forgiven Community

Admission by forgiveness only. Biblical faith insists that sinful
man comes back to God on the basis of God's gracious forgiveness. One may join human religious societies in many ways.
Entrance requirements range from "very strict" to "almost none
at all." But, one may join a "church" only if he comes by way
of the awareness of God, consciousness of his own sin, repentance, confession, and faith which issue in God's forgiveness.[2]
Consequently, the church is composed of "forgiven sinners."
Forgiveness is reconciliation to God and men. As has been
indicated in discussing the individual's experience of forgiveness, this is a very personal experience. It cannot be done by
proxy. The consciousness of personal sin, and the forgiveness
of it prepare one for entrance into the community of faith;
nothing else does.

Life within the church. The Christian life is the life of forgiveness and forgiving. Christians endure only because their forgiveness is repeated when they sin (1 John 1:9). They sustain erring
members by forgiving them (Eph. 4:32; Col. 3:13). Every time
Christians worship, they confess their sins and accept forgiveness. The Lord's Supper, the most sacred of their celebrations,
reminds them that their sin was so dreadful that Christ died for
them. They drink the wine with the understanding based on
Christ's statement, "This is my blood of the covenant, which
is poured out for many for the forgiveness of sins."

A living example. The church is a living example of God's
forgiveness. Men in sin, living under the curse and loneliness
of estrangement from God, gain hope merely by looking at the

church and knowing that these persons have been forgiven. H. R. Mackintosh pointed out that non-Christian neighbors begin to see the believability of Christian faith when they see their Christian neighbors receiving and practicing forgiveness. In his judgment, the most obvious failure of the church is its failure to forgive.[3]

A Christian distinctive. The recognition of sin and the humility to forgive and be forgiven mark off the Christian community from the legalistic Pharisaic community of Jesus' day. The church composed of the followers of Jesus are like the penitent publican and the prodigal son; the other religious communities have members who are like the Pharisee and the older brother.

The publican was conscious of his sin; in humility, he confessed and was forgiven. The prodigal son became aware of his sin, returned, confessed, and accepted forgiveness. The church is composed of people with a spirit like this, capable of acknowledging sin and accepting forgiveness.

Legalistic religion, even if found in a church wearing a Christian label, is like that of the Pharisee and the older brother. The Pharisee was so concerned with his own religious achievement that he boasted that he was not like other men. His self-righteousness was a highly developed form of sin as pride. It was religious pride. The older brother had no compassion for a "sinner." He desired no reconciliation with him, but the father did. Jesus clearly intended to contrast the Christian spirit with the Pharisaic spirit when he told these two stories. The church is distinctive in its doctrine, spirit, and practice of forgiveness.

Modern day "churches" should take stock of their own distinctive character with reference to forgiveness. Some "churches" have no place for the outcasts of society; some reject entire races; others reject people from lower social levels. Clubs may do this; churches cannot. Churches are communities of forgiven sinners; when sinners repent, they must be accepted joyfully, no questions asked.

A reminder. The Old Testament writers always called God's people to repentance by reminding them of God's wondrous acts in the past and the fact of judgment. This practice, sound in principle, has always helped to motivate God's people to faithfulness. The Ephesians were reminded that at one time they, "were dead through the trespasses and sins," and that they were "separated from Christ, alienated from the commonwealth of Israel, and strangers . . . having no hope and without God in the world." But, now, because of Christ's work, they stand as God's children (Eph. 2:1–22). We Christians need to be reminded often that we are "forgiven" sinners. We need to be reminded that apart from God's forgiveness we would be estranged.

The church is a community of forgiveness. As long as it remembers that fact, it can be a church. If it forgets, it can fall into the same sins into which individuals fall. If it seeks to elevate itself and perpetuate itself at all costs, does it not display the inordinate self-love so characteristic of the sin of pride? If it seeks to accumulate wealth and impressive buildings, does it not run the risk of elevating "world" to the rank of idolatry? If it loses itself in some noble cause, while forgetting its primary relationship to God, has it not committed the sin of sensuality? If the church remembers that it is the community of forgiven men and in the business of forgiving others, it is the true Christian community of reconciliation—the church.

The Church—The Forgiving Community

The forgiven are required to forgive. In the chapter "Forgiveness in the New Testament," we noted that Jesus taught that forgiving others is a requirement for being forgiven. He explained the particular statement of the Model Prayer (Matt.

6:14–15; Mark 11:25), and told the parable of the unmerciful servant (Matt. 18:23–35). The forgiven are required to forgive others "seven times in a day" (Luke 17:4) or "seventy times seven" times (Matt. 18:21–22).

The forgiven are disposed to forgive. The followers of Christ know the art of being gracious to those who sin. They forgive one another simply because Christ has forgiven them (Eph. 4:31–32; Col. 3:12 f.).

Even in serious problems of church discipline, the final solution is forgiveness. The majority in the church had imposed punishment on a sinning member. Neither the offense nor the punishment was specifically identified, but Paul wrote, in the true Christian spirit, "to forgive and comfort him, or he may be overwhelmed by excessive sorrow" (2 Cor. 2:7). Then Paul encouraged the Corinthians "to reaffirm your love for him," and indicated his own forgiveness of the person. Forgiving erring church members is the ultimate Christian solution. Forgiveness is essential in Christian life.

The forgiven and the keys of the kingdom. One very difficult but significant passage in the New Testament relates the church to the forgiveness of sins. After Peter's great confession at Caesarea Philippi, Jesus said, ". . . you are Peter, and on this rock I will build my church, and the powers of death shall not prevail against it. I will give you the keys of the kingdom of heaven, and whatever you bind on earth shall be bound in heaven, and whatever you loose on earth shall be loosed in heaven" (Matt. 16:18 f.).

The Roman Church, throughout much of its history, has interpreted this passage to teach the primacy of Peter and the authority of the Roman Church to forgive sins or to refuse to do so. Other Christian groups have rejected this interpretation as incompatible with the spirit and teachings of the New Testament. For instance, in the immediate context of this passage (Matt. 18:1 ff.), when the disciples asked "Who is the greatest in the kingdom of heaven?" Jesus replied by calling a small child to him and thereby indicating that the greatest is the humblest. On another occasion, when the mother of Zebedee's sons specifically requested priority for her sons, Jesus expressly refused the request and prohibited such "exercise" of "authority" as that later claimed for Peter. Jesus said, "It shall not be so among you." (See Matt. 20:20–28.) Consequently, it is quite unthinkable that Jesus intended to imply that the "keys of the kingdom" and the "binding" and "loosing" should be tied to such a view of Peter's authority so that he (or his successors) could admit to or exclude from heaven. But, it remains a fact that the passage definitely deals with the forgiveness of sins.

That "binding" and "loosing" have to do with the forgiveness of sins is obvious in two other passages. In a later chapter of the same Gospel (Matt. 18:15–20), Jesus gave instructions for the settlement of disputes among brethren. After other efforts failed, he advised, "tell it to the church." Then he repeated the statement about "binding" and "loosing" and concluded his statement by saying, "For where two or three are gathered in my name, there am I in the midst of them." Quite obviously, Jesus is not talking about the church in the sense of councils, business meetings, or authoritative decrees, but rather the reality in the fellowship of God's people in which eternal decisions are made. In the very next sentence, Peter established that the subject under discussion was in fact the forgiveness of sins; he asked, "Lord, how often shall my brother sin against me, and I forgive him? As many as seven times?" Jesus responded, ". . . seventy times seven" (Matt. 18:21 f.). The other passage is John 20:23. The risen Lord breathed on the disciples and told them to receive the Holy Spirit. Then he said, "If you forgive the sins of any, they are forgiven; if you retain the sins of any, they are retained." These passages indicate that decisions made by men and women in response to, or in the fellowship of, the message of the church are eternally binding. They are binding in heaven;

they have been "anticipated"[4] in heaven.

The church is not an authoritarian institution; it does not have the franchise on forgiveness of sins; it does not arbitrarily, or by decree, admit or forbid men and women to God's presence. The church is the people of God, the body of Christ, the community of the Holy Spirit, and the fellowship of forgiveness. The church has been entrusted with the message and mission of reconciliation (forgiveness) and by its ministry does business for God (2 Cor. 5:19–21). When it fails to minister to men for God, men and women remain in their sins, outside.

The "rock," or foundation, on which the church stands is not a man or his successors; rather, it is his confession of faith,[5] or the truth of that confession that Jesus is "the Christ, the Son of the living god" (Matt. 16:16). The "keys" and the "binding" and "loosing" indeed have to do with the forgiveness of sins, but in the sense of bringing the message of forgiveness and the spirit of forgiving.

Martin Luther clearly saw the "keys" as related to the forgiveness of sins and related to the passages cited.[6] John Calvin understood these passages to stress the forgiveness of sins within the church brought about through ministry.[7] Paul Tillich, in the Protestant tradition, said that the keys are the power of the "forgiveness of sins."[8]

It is quite unthinkable that Jesus, who rejected the kind of authority subsequently claimed for Peter and refused to give it to his disciples, would have set up such an institution. It is, however, fearfully true that he gave to his disciples the Word and ministry of reconciliation, which is "the forgiveness of sins." Churches, in their faithful ministry to men, point them to the open doors of heaven and show them how to enter. Chruches, in their failure to proclaim the gospel of forgiveness, leave men outside. The church must accept its responsibility, not as a privilege to be presumed upon, but as a ministry to be undertaken in fear and trembling.

The Ministry of Forgiveness

Those persons who are already in the Body of Christ should affirm with dedication and humility: "My church is a family of forgiveness, a channel through which God's forgiveness of sins passes on to men and women of every sort. We do not control forgiveness; we pass it on."

Proclaiming the message of forgiveness. The church holds the gospel in trust. It is the good news of God's forgiveness of sins. Multitudes of men and women near the churches are burdened down with sin and guilt. Lives are thwarted; homes are in shambles; hope is gone. The churches proclaim the joyful message, "Your sins can be forgiven!" The lives of the Christians provide convincing evidence that the promise is true. History is illuminated by the brightness of the lives of those who have responded to that message. No other human organization or institution can mediate such life-transforming power to burdened people. What doth hinder us?

An open door to sinners. It should be unnecessary to state that a church proclaiming this message must be prepared to admit those who respond. This should be quite natural and joyful for a true church. As did the Master, Christians rejoice in the forgiveness and healing of the harlots, alcoholics, addicts, and other outcasts for a million reasons. This attitude of rejoicing in the forgiveness of sinners should motivate "sinners" to say, "I will arise and go to the church; there they will understand and forgive me." It is regrettable that some churches have been converted into country clubs and have an unwritten sign in front which says "Restricted Clientele." The restriction usually means that we admit only those who are "like we are." Many modern churches have learned to their dismay that after preaching the gospel of forgiveness, and supporting a missionary endeavor to the world, they have been unable to "accept" those who responded and were forgiven. An attitude of acceptance, forgiving, and being forgiven must remain a part of the Christian consciousness.

Primary concern for persons. We have noted that God is personal (a significant aspect of man's "image of God" is his personal nature), that sin is personal breach, and that forgiveness is personal reconciliation. The church which would engage in the ministry of forgiveness must give priority to persons. This seems so obvious as to need no mention, but unfortunately, churches often confuse principles and persons. Usually, in controversy, persons are expendable and principles are inviolable. Institutions tend to perpetuate themselves; they will sacrifice persons for "principles." Most controversial issues are camouflaged by principles, even though they may be primarily personal in nature. Whenever churches practice "discipline," they usually miss the point of the New Testament. They punish someone for violating a church rule or, more often, for interfering with administrative smoothness. They do it in the name of "principle." The discipline known in the New Testament aims at the forgiveness of the person.

Forgiving its own. We have noted the forgiveness for sins committed by Christians, and their need for forgiving one another. The community of faith, a church, has a heavy responsibility to forgive its own. Many people, with years of experience in the church are burdened down with guilt; they have heard one part of the gospel, but have been denied its forgiveness. Many emotional problems seem to have been caused or encouraged by such preaching and teaching. The church is obliged to translate its message of forgiveness into the life of its members. Often, a church is more concerned for its own reputation than for the lives of those who constitute its membership.

In one instance, a young woman had brought embarrassment upon her family and church. She confessed privately to those involved and was forgiven. She continued her participation in the life of the congregation. Some years later, a retired minister, who had preached the gospel of forgiveness for decades, brought public criticism against members of the church staff for permitting her to sing in the public worship service. He was allegedly upholding some standard of morality. In a moment of forgetting, he had reverted to a pre-Christian faith. As a Christian man, he would have said quietly to himself as she sang: That young woman would have been lost except for this church family; we forgave her, and thereby redeemed both her and ourselves.

Practicing forgiveness. The term "practicing" should not be understood in the athletic sense of "getting ready" for the real contest. Rather, it should be understood in the way it is used by medical and legal specialists. With professional training behind them, they "practice" medicine and law. They already are skilled, but they are still learning. They subject their mistakes and successes to critical evaluation; thereby, they can "practice" more effectively.

Whether a church is seen as an institution, an organization, a family, or an expression of the body of Christ, it is a church only if it is true to its nature and mission. It is a forgiven community; its mission is to bring forgiveness of sin to men and women; its message is the gospel of forgiveness; its ministry is the ministry of reconciliation—the forgiveness of sins. Disinterested bystanders, when looking at those in the church, should be prompted to exclaim, "Behold, how they forgive one another!"

NOTES

1. H. R. Mackintosh, *The Christian Experience of Forgiveness* (London: Nisbet and Company, Ltd., 1927), p. 271.

2. John Calvin, *Institutes of the Christian Religion* Book IV, Chapter I, Section 20 (Philadelphia: The Westminster Press, 1960).

3. Mackintosh, *op. cit.,* p. 279.

4. Frank Stagg, "Matthew," *The Broadman Bible Commentary,* "(Nashville; Broadman Press, 1969), p. 175.

5. A. H. M'Neile, *The Gospel According to St. Matthew,* (London: Macmillan and Co., Limited, 1949), p. 241; T. H. Robinson, *The Gospel of Matthew,* "Moffatt New Testament Commentary," (New York and London: Harper and Brothers Publishers, 1927), p. 141.

6. Martin Luther, "On The Papacy In Rome," *Luther's Works,* Ed. Eric W. Gritsch (Philadelphia: Fortress Press, 1970), Vol. 39, p. 86 f.

7. Calvin, *op. cit.,* Book IV, Chap. i, Sect. 22.

8. Paul Tillich, *A History of Christian Thought* (Ed. Carl E. Braaten) (New York and Evanston: Harper & Row, 1968), p. 232 f.

VIII
FORGIVENESS IN RESPONSE TO CRITICISMS AND QUESTIONS

There are several theological objections to the doctrine of the forgiveness of sin. I shall attempt to summarize them under four headings and offer some response to each. The numerous questions most often asked are both practical and theological in nature and usually grow out of some misunderstanding of forgiveness. I shall state them and respond briefly to each.

Theological Criticisms

Forgiveness is impossible. The argument is as follows: God is the creator of the universe and has endowed it with his own moral character; man has sinned against God; sin brings inevitable consequences; man must stand before God and be judged for his sin; therefore, forgiveness is impossible since it would violate the nature of God, man, and the universal moral law. One must suffer the consequences of his sin.

The criticism appears weighty, but it is based upon at least four theological misunderstandings, at least from the Christian viewpoint: the doctrine of God, the meaning of law, the biblical view of judgment, and the biblical understanding of forgiveness.

In biblical faith, God is more than moral judge. He is heavenly Father. His nature is holy love; he is free; he is sovereign; he cares for his creatures. The criticism appears to subordinate God to an eternal law. The law is not an inviolable order of creation; it is a statement of what God expects of his creatures; it is not a limitation on God.

Judgment is not only punishment for sin, though it may

include that. The judgment of God also acquits man if he is not guilty. Repentance and confession of sin constitute man's willing acceptance of God's judgment. In the experience of salvation, man is judged; he acknowledges his guilt; God in Christ justifies him or acquits him.

The most obvious misunderstanding underlying the criticism is its view of forgiveness, which apparently means only the remission of penalty or consequences. Forgiveness is primarily personal reconciliation to God and to other men.

If God is the personal Father of our Lord Jesus Christ and if forgiveness of sin is reconciliation to God and men, forgiveness is indeed possible through faith in Christ.

Forgiveness is immoral. This criticism is essentially the same as the former. It proceeds in this manner. God has stated: "Be sure your sin will find you out" (Num. 32:23) and "Do not be deceived; God is not mocked, for whatever a man sows, that he will also reap" (Gal. 6:7). All men are sinners against God, so the inevitable consequences are universal. But, although *all* are sinners, *some* are forgiven; that is immoral. If God has made exceptions to his moral law by forgiving some persons, and others suffer for their sins, he has acted unjustly, immorally. Since this is unthinkable, we must revert to the previous assertion that forgiveness is impossible.

The response to this criticism is adequately stated in the previous response; there is little difference. But, one should note how legalistic the views of God and man are. There is no appreciation for the "personal" nature of God or man; there is, therefore, no appreciation for forgiveness as personal reconciliation. In such a legalistic setting, forgiveness means only remission of penalities (punishment), and even that is undesirable and unjust. How different in contrast to the Christian understanding of forgiveness of sin!

In the light of God as revealed in Jesus Christ, man is a creature who does not retaliate for wrongs, but he forgives and prays for the wrongdoer as a means of bringing him to God. Reconciliation is Christian; rigid legalism is something else.

Forgiveness is license to sin. This criticism of forgiveness is usually stated: If God (or men) forgives sin freely and without punishment, men will regard sin lightly and will use forgiveness as a license for sinning. It was once stated by an older, wealthy, moral, religious church member, who stood up in a class on the parables of Jesus: "You preachers make forgiveness so attractive and easy, you actually encourage people to sin. I have always appreciated the older brother more than the prodigal son, anyway."

Those who argue that forgiveness of sin is license to sin betray a legalistic view of God and punishment. They insist that every man has a criminal mentality and wants to get away with all of the wickedness he can. They demonstrate that they do not know that forgiveness of sin is personal reconciliation. Their most serious misunderstanding is that their legalistic orientation causes them to overlook the personal transformation which takes place when a sinner becomes conscious of God's claim on his life, conscious of his own sin, and comes to repentance, confession, and faith.

One who has made the journey through the agony of guilt and repentance for his own sin into the joy of forgiveness-reconciliation with God and man may stumble into sin, but he is a "new creation"; he won't go back into sin if he can help it. A forgiven man does not have a "criminal mentality"; he has the "mind of Christ" (1 Cor. 2:16; see Phil. 2:5).

Forgiveness contradicts atonement. This objection is usually raised by those guarding a particular view of the atonement. I have discussed this at some length in the chapter "Forgiveness and the Forgiver." Briefly, the criticism can be stated in question form: How is the forgiveness of sin related to the death of Christ? or, If God forgave sin before Jesus came and Jesus forgave sin in his lifetime and if he commanded men to forgive, was the cross necessary for forgiveness? or, worst of all, If God expects men to forgive one another without a sacrifice or payment for sin, why did he require the death of Christ on the cross as the basis of forgiveness?

These questions betray a misunderstanding of the nature of God, a lack of appreciation for the true incarnation, the idea that forgiveness has to do solely with remission of punishment, and the erroneous idea that God was responsible for Christ's death.

This question vanishes when one considers the following themes: God was really in Christ; Christ was truly God and man; Christ showed us what God is like and what man ought to be; Christ called men to God, but evil men murdered him; the death of Christ on the cross brought God to men and men to God; forgiveness is genuine reconciliation to God and to men. Then, it means something to say "Christ died for us."

There are many questions about the cross which cannot be answered; mystery remains. But, the theme of incarnation with its personal disclosure of God suggests that our understanding of it should be in terms of personal interaction rather than in terms of legalism. Jesus spent quite a large percentage of his time trying to displace a legalistic religion. His teaching should point us away from such legalistic interpretations as those posed in the preceding objections.

The question about God demanding a sacrifice and man being required to forgive without such a sacrifice is nullified on two grounds: God did not "demand" a sacrifice but showed his love in sending Christ; the personal nature of God and man makes forgiveness a personal reconciliation whether it be between God and men or between men. Man forgives other men on the basis of Christ's forgiveness (see Col. 3:13).

Theological-Practical Questions

If God has forgiven me, why do I still suffer the consequences of sin? The person who asks this question is usually suffering from some previous decisions or actions and regards the suffering as a punishment for his sin. He has come to the awareness of God's forgiveness and, having been taught that forgiveness removes the consequences of sin, is disappointed in the incompleteness of forgiveness.

For instance, a father lived selfishly and immorally while his children were young. His behavior set a bad example before them and finally destroyed his home. Now, he has accepted God's forgiveness and is well on the way toward reconciliation with others. But, his wife married another; his children are living in the way he taught them. In his newfound joy of forgiveness, he cannot understand why others are not changed. Forgiveness does not restore the years the locusts have eaten. It restores the personal reconciliation with God and others.

Another man dissipated a fortune and his health in sinful living. Now that he is forgiven, he sees poverty and bad health as consequences of sin. He actually feels disappointment that forgiveness does not restore all.

The idea of punishment or consequences for sin is an oversimplification for many of the experiences of life. One should exercise caution in interpreting all of the ills of life as punishment for sin. The problem is more complex; in some instances, the most devoted people of God appear to suffer more than others. Is it fair to interpret suffering in this manner when we see so little of the whole pattern of existence?

The reminder that forgiveness solves the personal problem of estrangement will help with the question. After one is right personally, he is in a position to work on the other problems. But, the surveyor determines the property line; the lawyer works out legal problems; the physician helps in matters of health. The student suspended from school for cheating will not automatically be reinstated, if and when he is forgiven by God; but, any indication of such a change in him will very likely be greeted with enthusiasm by the authorities who suspended him. The burden of presenting his case, however, is on him.

Lest forgiveness be minimized, it should be remembered that, while every person must work on many problems and live with unpleasant consequences of his own actions, that of others, and of those which attend the generation in which he lives, the forgiven man can face life now that he is right with God, with others, and with himself.

If God has forgiven me, why won't others forgive me? This question is very painful to him who asks it. In some instances, the appraisal is correct and other people will not forgive him even though God has. In some instances, they don't need to forgive, because there has been no personal breach. On occasions, he mistakes lack of respect for unwillingness to forgive. The forgiven man often thinks forgiveness restores everything involved, but it deals primarily with the personal breach.

One must find a way to go on without resentment in spite of the awareness that some persons will not forgive. One should not expect "uninvolved" persons to "forgive" him; in most instances, no forgiveness is in order. After being forgiven, one may have to earn the respect he lost during the original problem. Lack of full respect is not the same as unwillingness to forgive.

This question more often reflects a confusion between forgiveness and the restoration of all losses related to the original forgiveness-situation. For instance, a young bank teller, and son-in-law of the bank president, took bank funds for personal use. When the shortage was discovered and the teller admitted what he had done, the bank president worked through both the personal sin and the crime with the teller in the best way that he could. The funds were restored; prosecution was avoided. Of course, he had to dismiss the teller. The older man contacted other business corporations and sought to assist the young man in finding a position which did not require handling money, a position for which he had disqualified himself. After the confrontation ended, the father-in-law said, "Helen and I will be expecting you and Margie Friday evening for dinner." Forgiveness had saved the personal relationship and had helped work out the other problems. But, if the bank president had not recognized that his son-in-law had disqualified himself to work in the bank, he would have been disqualified himself. Forgiveness solves personal problems; it is not a cloak for irresponsible action.

I can forgive others; why can't I accept forgiveness? This question reflects a serious inward condition. It is a fact that "accepting" forgiveness is quite difficult; in fact, it is more difficult than forgiving. But, one cannot really do one without being able to do the other. Jesus made it clear that one cannot be forgiven unless he forgives. Both forgiving and being forgiven hinge on a human awareness of sin, consciousness of human frailty, and the need for free grace.

The person who says he can forgive but cannot accept forgiveness is deceiving himself. In all probability, instead of forgiving others, he is rationalizing, explaining, or looking upon others as weaker than he. In fact, he condescendingly tolerates them but does not actually "forgive" them. He is incapable of forgiving if he is incapable of being forgiven. His basic problem is pride; pride is the inordinate self-love and self-assertion. This man cannot "accept" forgiveness because he cannot accept the fact that he is a sinner. To acknowledge, "I have sinned," annihilates my pride. Forgiveness is known only to the humble.

If God has forgiven me, why do I still feel guilty? This question is closely related to the former one. In other words, it says, Why can't I forgive myself?

A person refusing to forgive himself by still feeling guilty may be merely expressing his sinful pride. He cannot admit that he is really a sinner and, therefore, helpless. By feeling guilty, he refuses to be a creature of God and clings to his own self-centered existence.

Erroneous religious teaching often consigns persons to a lifetime of needless guilt. They have been taught that true repentance is feeling sorry for sins, and they go on feeling sorry for sin, for religious reasons, while they actually become emotionally unstable. Or, they have been so indoctrinated in the notion that sin has inevitable consequences, that they insist on suffering as a means of "deserving" forgiveness. Of course, this denies what forgiveness is. It also points out the serious consequences of erroneous religious instruction.

Another possibility is more serious. It is related to the previous one. In remaining guilty, refusing to forgive himself, a person may actually be inflicting punishment on himself. Instead of accepting the free forgiveness of God, he goes on cruelly exacting the punishment he thinks his sin deserves. Apart from the emotional and mental health implications, this man is doing something quite cruel. He usurps God's role in punishing; he subjects his family to living with a prisoner rather than with a joyful God-freed man; he confines himself to perpetual torment. And all of this he does needlessly, and even worse, in the name of serving the God who forgives. It would be criminal to punish another for a lifetime; on what ground can one justify his cruel punishment of himself? God forgives us; he expects us to live joyfully.

Can forgiveness remove guilt for temptation? No! Forgiveness deals with sin, but not with temptation. This question is usually not worded in this way. It arises out of the confusion of temptation with "sins of the heart." Because of this confusion, many people suffer needless guilt for sins they have not committed.

The ethic of Jesus is higher than that required by the law of Moses. Jesus indicated that his followers must be pure in heart. It is not enough for them to refrain from murder and adultery; they must not even hate or lust (Matt. 6:21–32). This teaching has been misunderstood by many to mean that one is guilty of murder in his heart if he even gets angry with another and

adultery in his heart if he even thinks about a sex experience
with someone other than his own spouse. If Jesus meant to
convey this understanding, who is not a murderer or adulterer?

A clue toward understanding is Jesus' own temptation: he
was tempted to use his power for personal reasons, to inaugurate
his kingdom with a sensational exhibition of his power, and to
achieve the kingdom of God by using the methods of the world
(Matt. 4:1–12). Unless he really "considered" it, it was not
temptation, and the Scripture says that Jesus "in every respect
has been tempted as we are, yet without sinning" (Heb. 4:15).
If Jesus had achieved his kingdom by employing the methods
of the world, he would have had not the kingdom of God but
another kingdom of this world. He struggled inwardly and rejected the temptation; he did not sin.

Everyone struggles inwardly against the hate and lust. If one
struggles to do right and overcomes his temptation, he has not
sinned; he needs no forgiveness; he should suffer no guilt. If,
however, one would go ahead and "kill" the person, or "commit
adultery," if he thought he could get away with it or if the law
didn't forbid it, he has done something quite evil. If he harbors
the hatred and comes to enjoy his passionate lust, he is guilty.
But, as long as he struggles against the temptation and with
God's help overcomes it, he should not feel guilty and needs
no forgiveness nor confession.

There was once a young man, trying diligently to be a "good"
Christian, who "confessed" to another man in the fellowship:
"I want to apologize to you; I looked upon your wife with desire.
I prayed to God to forgive me; I want you to forgive me."
Instead of accepting gratefully and privately the victory God
had given him over temptation, this foolish man advertised his
temptation in such a way as to endanger other persons. As long
as one struggles with his temptations and prevents them from
becoming acts of sin, he needs no forgiveness from God or men,
and he certainly cannot "confess" a sin he did not commit.

If God forgives me, must I make restitution? This question grows out of certain provisions in the Old Testament for paying debts and penalties if one had defrauded another. It should be unnecessary to state that saint and sinner, with or without religion or forgiveness, is expected to pay his debts and repay with interest his wrong dealings of the past. Minimum standards of law and decency require as much; a "forgiven man" could never do less. Forgiveness is not a license. But, we are not really discussing forgiveness.

Most of the damages and injuries resulting from our sins cannot be repaid. Most of them are in the personal lives of people; they are beyond reach. This is why forgiveness is personal reconciliation; it is a chance to start over without repaying all of the indebtedness of the past. A man who may have deeply injured a former wife in his sinning cannot go back and "make it up" to her; she may have married another. He cannot even talk to her, in most instances, without causing her further risk. He must accept the forgiveness of God and start over. But, if one can repair some of the damage he has done, he should certainly do so. This is one of the creative results of being forgiven.

Every responsible human being, and particularly the Christian man, must act responsibly in his dealings with others and must make restitution for his wrongs, if he can. Bankruptcy laws provide a way for an individual hopelessly in debt to go on. Of course, he should repay his debts, but he can't. The law permits declaration of bankruptcy as a means of letting him start over. If he later becomes financially solvent, although the law doesn't require it, he will repay those whom he owed if he is a fully responsible person.

If God forgives a man, must he reform morally? The question was worded by one who did not know the nature of the experience leading to forgiveness. Forgiven man wants to reform; that is why he repented. But, the question is frequently asked.

Several years ago, Dean Joergen Jensen of Denmark published a sermon in the Copenhagen newspaper, *Kristeligt Dagblad,* on the story of the woman of the streets recorded in Luke 7:36–50.[1] In the sermon, Jensen maintained that after being forgiven, the woman, of course, went back to her trade on the streets just the same as before. When objections were raised, the Bishop defended Jensen's interpretation of forgiveness and claimed that forgiveness was brought to her just as she was and indeed comes to all of us just as we are.

Of course the editors of *Christianity Today* argued against the interpretation of Jensen and the Bishop and were right in doing so. The basic fallacy in the original assertion is the failure to recognize the transforming power of the experience of forgiveness. It is true that one does not have to reform in order to be forgiven; he couldn't do it. It is also true that transformation is inevitable when one knows the forgiveness of God.

If one asks the question in an attempt to retain his former sinful ways, he indicates that he has not really known the consciousness of sin or repentance. To be sure, the forgiveness of sin results in change for the better.

Should I forgive someone who has not repented or confessed? This question is more often stated as an assertion, I will forgive him when he repents and confesses. This appears to mean, I won't forgive him until he does, and introduces an attitude into the situation that is foreign to the spirit of forgiving. Technically, it may be true that full forgiveness cannot be achieved until the guilty party has asked for forgiveness, but Jesus instructed the "offended" brother to take the initiative and go to the "offender" and seek reconciliation (Matt. 18:15).

Among those who pray for their enemies and go the second mile with the "demanders," a forgiving spirit can handle unpleasant situations apart from the technicalities of formal apologies and evidences of repentance.

What if I forgive but do not "forget"? One may quibble over the questions: Can one actually forget? or Should one forget? The terminology is used for emphasis. In "Forgiveness in the Old Testament," we noted that "forgiveness is forgetting sin." Jeremiah wrote, "I will forgive their iniquity, and I will remember their sin no more" (Jer. 31:34). The psalmist said, "as far as the east is from the west, so far does he remove our transgressions from us" (Psalm 103:12). The point is that God blots out sin; he holds no grudges. When we forgive, we should hold no grudges.

The question is not the theoretical question, Is it possible for one to forget—God or man? The question is: When I forgive a person, will I drop the issue and never bring it up again? Forget it if I can?

The assertion, "I will forgive him, but I'll keep my eye on him," means, "I won't forgive him at all." The ugly comment, made upon a repetition of the offense, "I forgave him, but I didn't expect him to do any better next time," is translated to mean, "I didn't forgive him in the first place; I have held a grudge against him, and now I am proved right."

If I genuinely forgive another, I must "forget" the sin; I must not call it back to mind for his sake and my own. Ritschl argued that it is impossible to remove the memory of guilt, and that such memory gives meaning to forgiveness. He argued that the consciousness of guilt and pain are removed, leaving only the memory of it.[2] But Ritschl was speaking of my memory of my sin, not the memory of sins of others whom I have forgiven.

What is the unpardonable sin? It is not likely that a person "concerned" about the unpardonable sin has committed it. The attitude of interest is concern enough to justify the assertion of innocence. The "unforgivable sin" is identified in the Gospels as blasphemy against the Holy Spirit (Mark 3:29–30; Matt. 12: 22–32). Other biblical passages are sometimes cited as being related to the unpardonable sin, or the "eternal" sin (2 Thess. 1:8 f.; Heb. 6:4–6; 10:26–31; 1 John 5:14–17).

In the Gospel passage, Jesus had healed a demoniac. The religious leaders accused Jesus of doing the wonder in the power of Beelzebub (prince of demons). In other words, when confronted with a work of God through the power of the Holy Spirit, they attributed it to the work of Satan. This cannot be a casual comment nor an act done in haste or without thinking. This is a deeply ingrained spiritual wickedness resulting in blindness. It is "unforgivable" not because God has arbitrarily decreed it so, but because by its commission one renders himself unforgivable; he willfully closes the only door open to his forgiveness.[3] The Holy Spirit leads to repentance; to blaspheme the Holy Spirit is to deny oneself access to forgiveness.

In the light of the repeated biblical emphasis on repentance and forgiveness, it is reasonable to assume that man is forgivable and that God desires to forgive him. One should respond to the invitation to forgiveness; he should not worry about the unforgivable sin; he should respond in reverence to the name of Holy Spirit, Father, and Son.

NOTES

1. "Beyond Forgiveness," *Christianity Today,* November 6, 1964, p. 31 f.

2. Albrecht B. Ritschl, *The Christian Doctrine of Justification and Reconciliation.* Edited by H. R. Mackintosh and A. B. Macaulay (Clifton, N.J.: Reference Book Publishers, 1966), p. 53.

3. See Frank Stagg, "Matthew," and Henry E. Turlington, "Mark," *The Broadman Bible Commentary* (Nashville: Broadman Press, 1969), Vol. 8, pp. 149, 293 f.

IX
FORGIVENESS AND THE CREATIVE POWER OF FORGIVING

According to Genesis, before the creation of the world only God was. God created everything. God said, "Let there be . . . and there was. . . ." By his act of will and word, God created the world out of nothing. The forgiveness of sin is like creation. By his will and word, God says, "Your sins are forgiven!" They are no more. Previously, they were; they were barriers, like mountains, between God and men, between men and men; God wills them out of existence. Before his creative word, they vanish like the morning fog before the rising sun. They marred man's life like deep indelible stains; God's word of forgiving washes them as white as snow. They were on the record books as condemning evidence against man; God spoke the word of forgiveness and blotted them out. Sins were "something"; God forgave; they are nothing at all.

As a sinner, God's own creature lived alone in a strange and hostile land only faintly remembering the destiny from which he had fallen. He was surrounded by others like himself but estranged from them. God forgave man and he was suddenly restored to God who made him, and to the fellowmen among whom he had lived a lonely, alienated life. Forgiveness makes him a child of God and a brother to other men. Worship and community result from forgiveness. This is a new creation out of nothing, out of chaos.

God has not only given man the power to forgive other men, he has also commanded that man do so. In the act of forgiving, man exercises a creative power like that of God in whose image he was created. James G. Emerson, Jr., has spoken of this as "realized forgiveness," and says that man has the freedom to be a "new creature" as well as a "new creator." [1] Forgiving may be the most "creative" act man ever accomplishes. Without detracting from the creativity required to write a great poem, paint a great scene, or build a great cathedral, consider what forgiving creates. A man by an act of will lifts another from the miry clay of guilt and sets his feet upon a rock. By forgiving, one individual sets forces in motion which revolutionize and transform a family from a group of estranged individuals into a community of persons which encourages creative living. Forgiving, in one personal act of will, can blot out a diseased and destructive situation and create a new environment in which persons live and work. Forgiving is creative.

A Review

God created man as a person; he set him in a context of meaningful relationships under God, with men, and over nature. God gave man genuine freedom; he set him in dominion over nature; he made man responsible both to God and to his human situation, both present and future.

Man sinned. He misused his freedom for no reason at all. He exalted himself against God who created him; he rebelled, he distrusted God, he loved himself inordinately, he fell. This sin became universal among men; it spread its malignancy into every area of individual and social life. It disrupted the entire creation: man lost sight of the personal nature of God, and thereafter depersonalized himself and others. He exchanged his structure of relationships for estrangement from God and men so that now a man can kill his brother and respond when interrogated, "Am I my brother's keeper?" In sin, freedom ceases, and man becomes a slave to demonic powers within and numerous powers without. As sinner, instead of ruling over nature under God, man exploits nature, idolizes some part of it, or loses the distinction between himself and nature. Sinful man does not respond to God or to his fellowmen "responsibly" but denies his accountability and thinks only of himself.

God's only solution for man's sin is forgiveness. God calls man to come through repentance and faith to forgiveness. God's forgiveness restores man to his intended role as existence in the "image of God." Reconciliation restores: man now sees God as personal heavenly Father and men as creatures for whom Christ died. Joyfully, he lives in the intended relationships under God, with men, and over and responsible for nature. Again, he accepts life in freedom with all the risks and possibilities which frighten. As ruler of nature, he destroys his idols, puts nature to its proper use, and begins the almost hopeless task of repairing the damage done by his exploitation. Forgiven man is responsible again in that he "responds" to God and to his human situation with accountability. This is a new creation.

In Forgiving, God Creates

A forgiven man is a new creation. John called it a "new birth" (John 3:7), and Paul called it a "new creation" (2 Cor. 5:17; Gal. 6:15). Man was possessed by demonic powers; now, he is free. He knew about God but was estranged from him; now, he knows God and is obedient to him. He used other people and was used by them; now, they form a community of persons. He lived for himself; now, he lives for God and for his fellowmen, accounting to them. Once, he loved himself most of all; now, he loves other men and really cares for them. Once, he lived under the bondage of guilt for all of this wrong he knew but would not acknowledge; now, in liberation, he is free—a new creature.

The forgiven community is new creation. God's forgiveness creates a new community of men. The self-centered man now enters a community of forgiven-reconciled men. At first, he may feel strange, but pride gives way to worship, and self-centeredness gives way to love for neighbor. This new environment is a new creation. Life is integrated around God and with men. In this setting, man feels the creative power of God. God continues his creation in this community. Men distorted by sin are re-created in the "image of God."

In Forgiving, Man Creates

Individual forgiving. Forgiving others is an inseparable part of being forgiven. Forgiving another is an act of creation.

When a man forgives another for a wrong, he removes from that person the load of guilt. He creates a new situation for him in which the man can live and earn his daily bread. It gives him hope and a new relationship which inspires him to genuinely personal living. It removes from his back a useless and heavy burden so that he can assume the right burden. Forgiving him restores him to a small community of persons in which, and only in which, he can live responsibly. Forgiving him elevates him to personal existence; ignoring, forgetting, tolerating, or "explaining him" reduces him to the role of a thing. One can commit a kind of murder by refusing to forgive another person. He can wipe out the personal existence of another. But, in forgiving him one does something creative for that person.

Forgiving another man does something creative in the life of the forgiver. Not only has he removed a burden from the back of another, he has also removed a heavy burden from his own back. Few burdens are more galling than the grudge. Forgive him and lighten your own load!

When an individual creatively forgives another, he often saves a whole family. Many families, distressed by estrangement, fragment into hostile camps. The resultant environment poisons the air for all members. One person can often save the entire family by one creative act of forgiving. This act transforms the group into a family of healthy relationships.

An individual participates in numerous collectives of other

human beings: the club, church, labor union, political party, shop crew, or office personnel. These collectives come to know a corporate life and are influenced by the persons who share in them. Often, one forgiving person can creatively prevent, or solve, a score of potential problems which could disrupt and destroy. Forgiveness is creative; it prevents or cures chaos. In such groups, there is always the danger of depersonalization of persons. Individuals who know forgiveness and how to forgive add a creative power in areas of personal relationships.

Church as creative forgiver. The church is the forgiven and forgiving community. It proclaims the message of and demonstrates forgiveness to the world. As a forgiving family, it forgives its members and teaches them how to live the free and personal life of the forgiven. Only in this way can they respond to the challenges of life. Otherwise, they exhaust their energies bearing the false burden of pride and guilt. It is a terrible and unjust sentence to go through life carrying a burden for guilt. God has offered forgiveness. The church must proclaim to us, "Your sins are forgiven! Lay down the burden of guilt! Take up your cross, and follow Christ!"

The church does something very creative when it teaches men how to forgive others. Then, they go into their homes, to their jobs, and to other human collectives, forgiving and teaching others to forgive. In this way, the church is the "salt of the earth" and "light of the world." Its ministry is not limited to its own members; it has a creative ministry to the whole world.

Other institutions have other ways. The state can seek to correct offenders by punishment, fines, or confinement. The church can forgive and restore offenders to responsible personhood. The church cares, loves, and forgives. Through creative discipline it seeks the restoration of its worst offenders. Creative forgiveness is redemptive. No other institution is so well equipped to introduce forgiveness of sins into the world. There is much joy in doing so. The creative power is immeasurable!

Why are we so grudging?

The apostle Paul wrote, "All this is from God, who through Christ reconciled us to himself and gave us the ministry of reconciliation; that is, God was in Christ reconciling the world to himself. . . . We are ambassadors for Christ" (2 Cor. 5: 18–20).

"As the Lord has forgiven you, so you also must forgive" (Col. 3:13).

NOTES

1. James G. Emerson, Jr., *The Dynamics of Forgiveness* (Philadelphia: The Westminster Press, 1964), p. 21.

APPENDIX

In the previous chapters, I have tried to present the biblical, theological, and practical ideas on the forgiveness of sin. In my judgment, many people, Christian and otherwise, are suffering needlessly because of the lack of forgiveness. At least some of them would be helped by practical preaching and teaching on the subject. In this appendix, I suggest a number of themes which could be developed and illustrated so as to make very helpful sermons or lessons on forgiveness. It is my conviction that we would be serving the Lord faithfully if we teach men and women how to accept forgiveness and how to forgive. I propose sermons on the "Neglected Themes and Implications of Forgiveness."

"Forgiveness Is Born of Love"

"How can I give you up, O Ephraim!"

"When Israel was a child, I loved him, and out of Egypt I called my son. The more I called them, the more they went from me; . . . How can I give you up, O Ephraim!" (Hos. 11:1–8).

Forgiveness is the child of love. It is born only in the personal relationship in which people "care" about other persons. The meaning of forgiveness has almost been lost in the context of legalism in which people lay down prerequisites and conditions of forgiveness. Hosea loved his wife Gomer even though she was a harlot. In spite of her unfaithfulness, he loved her so much he would not "give her up." In this domestic tragedy, Hosea learned how it was between God and his people. God loved his people; they were unfaithful; God loved them so much that he forgave them. The motivation was not their worth, actual or potential. Their forgiveness was an act of sheer grace; God just loved them.

In Luke 15, God says a great deal about forgiveness. The forgiving father had two sons. He loved them both. The younger son rebelled against the father, rejected the instruction of his youth, and wasted resources belonging to the family. But, the father loved him so much that he would not "let him go" even though he had left home. Later, when the son thought of returning home, he remembered his father's love. When he returned, the father showed his love in genuine and full forgiveness.

God's love is qualitatively different from ordinary human love. Men tend to love the lovely; they expect a "return" or a "reward" for their love. Human love is motivated by value, potential, or expectation from the person or object loved. Even a mother's love has an element of selfishness in it. But God's love *(agapé)* does not rest on so unsure a foundation. He loves because of who he is—not because of what we are or may become. "God shows his love for us in that while we were yet sinners Christ died for us" (Rom. 5:8). Jesus said, "This is my commandment, that you love one another as I have loved you" (John 15:12).

Forgiving others is not so difficult if we first understand the nature of Christian love. The question is not whether the person deserves another chance, or whether he has repented. Rather, the question is, "Do I really care for him?" In his story about the "woman of the city" who anointed Jesus with ointment and washed his feet with her tears, Jesus indicated that there is a direct ratio between forgiveness and love (Luke 7:47).

In a superb little book, *Love, Power, and Justice,* Paul Tillich points out that love uses power to achieve justice. In person-to-person encounters, only love can accomplish justice because love "listens," is "giving," and "forgiving."

Love takes the first step in forgiving. It is never passive; it is always active. The shepherd who lost the sheep left the other ninety-nine and went out to seek the one that was lost. The woman who lost the coin actively sought for it until she found it. The forgiving father of the prodigal son "while he was yet at a distance . . . saw him . . . and ran and embraced him" (Luke 15:20). This father did not wait for apologies; he met his son. The prodigal son was motivated more by the memory of his father's love than by his own desperate condition. Jesus was quite specific in teaching his disciples that the offended person should not wait for the offender to come seeking forgiveness, but rather that he take the initiative and seek out the offender so that forgiveness may be achieved.

Genuine Christian love transcends the legalistic limits which bind us. Love begets forgiveness. Men who know God's love can and will forgive others. They will also introduce God's love and forgiveness to others. Christian love will cause Christians to say to the unreconciled, "How can I give you up!" Love will find a way to achieve forgiveness.

"Forgiveness Is an Occasion for Joy"

Few aspects of forgiveness are more neglected than the element of joy. And this is strange because the biblical texts usually stress the rejoicing which accompanies or follows forgiveness.

"Blessed is he whose transgression is forgiven, whose sin is covered. . . . Be glad in the Lord, and rejoice, O righteous, and shout for joy, all you upright in heart!" (Ps. 32:1,11).

"Fill me with joy and gladness; let the bones which thou has broken rejoice. . . . Restore to me the joy of thy salvation." (Ps. 51:8,12).

"Even so, I tell you, there is joy before the angels of God over one sinner who repents. . . . It was fitting to make merry and be glad, for this your brother was dead, and is alive; he was lost, and is found." (Luke 15:10,32).

Happiness is being forgiven; happiness is being able to forgive; happiness is observing people forgive one another. The biblical word "blessed" comes through in English better in the word

"happy." "Happy is he whose transgression is forgiven. . . ."
Even in the beatitudes of our Lord, the word "happy" catches
the intended meaning and spirit. "Happy are the poor in spirit
. . . Happy are the meek. . . ." Happiness is never something
one gets by seeking or achieving; it is always a by-product of
something else. It is the joyful result of being right with God
and men.

In the light of so many biblical emphases on joy, it is amazing
that contemporary religion has lost much of the element of
celebration in worship. The Bible speaks of rejoicing, singing,
celebrating, giving thanks, and praise. The Hebrews had twenty-
seven words (built on thirteen roots) to express their joyful
participation in religious activities. Perhaps, we moderns have
confused the great drama of forgiveness with the gloomy background of sin and guilt against which it is cast. To be sure sin
and guilt are depressing, but forgiveness is joyful liberation from
this defeat. Many people confuse repentance with sorrow. They
say that repentance is being sorry for sin, but this is not an
adequate statement about repentance in the Bible. It is the
turning to God. There is a kind of sorrow for sin which leads
only to death (2 Cor. 7:10), but godly sorrow for sin leads to
repentance which is a joyful turning to God. Jesus preached
repentance on the basis of a joyful expectation. He said, "The
time is fulfilled, and the kingdom of God is at hand; repent, and
believe in the gospel." In other words, it is a joyful occasion
and one must not miss it.

Forgiveness of sin is the joyful experience of liberation. One
is liberated from bondage to sin, guilt, and wrong. One is reconciled to God and fellowmen. As such, it is an occasion for
celebration. The homecoming of the prodigal demands a banquet; victory over sin calls for a victory celebration; forgiveness
is healing and healing always brings rejoicing.

The angels in heaven rejoice when a sinner repents; a father
rejoices when he gets to forgive a wayward son; the church

praises God when a sinner accepts forgiveness. The Christian life is a victorious life of joy and celebration. Individual Christians find their greatest occasion for joy when they see other persons redeemed through forgiveness and restored to God and other men.

"Happy is he whose transgression is forgiven!"

"Forgiveness Is an Act of Justice"

One of the most persistent criticisms of forgiveness is that it is unjust. The accusation is sometimes stated in the term "immoral." Always the charge reflects some standard or law which has been violated and must be kept inviolate. We have noted how this error is avoided if we remember the personal nature of forgiveness and reject the legalistic interpretation. Those who would refuse to forgive and would camouflage their lack of forgiveness in the name of justice are legion. Their biblical guide is the older brother (Luke 15:25–32).

Accusingly, he spoke to his father upon the return of the prodigal son: "Lo, these many years I have served you, and I never disobeyed your command; yet you never gave me a kid, that I might make merry with my friends. But when this son of yours came, who has devoured your living with harlots, you killed for him the fatted calf!" In other words, "Unfair! Unjust! It isn't fair!"

He betrayed his stance for justice when he referred to his brother as "this son of yours." No fraternal love sneaks through that phrase. It is like the estranged wife who while seeking counsel from her pastor repeatedly refers to her husband as "that man." There is not much hope here. The unforgiving older brother forgets persons and conceals his cruelty by assuming the role of defending principles.

The older brother appears to have had a legitimate complaint against the younger brother's handling of money and some provision may have been in order to safeguard the family in the future. But, rejecting his brother was wrong. Criticizing his father's forgiveness was cruel.

The father's response, "It was fitting to make merry and be glad, for this your brother was dead, and is alive; he was lost, and is found" says in substance, "what I have done is right. He is my son; I am his father; it was right for me to forgive him." He implied that it would have been right for the older brother to have done the same.

The parables of Luke 15 were grouped together and related to criticism by the Pharisees and scribes. The parables portray the love and forgiveness of God in contrast to the legalistic outlook of the opponents. The obvious intent is that any shepherd would seek a lost sheep, any woman would search for a lost coin, and any father would cherish the opportunity of receiving a wayward son back home. The older brother portrays a legalistic mentality as opposed to the distinctly "Christian" attitude which is always oriented around persons.

The word "justice" in contemporary usage often has the legalistic connotation. In the Bible, the word "just" means "right." "Justice is righteousness." The righteous man is one who does right. The forgiving father maintained that his act of forgiving his son was right. It was an act of justice. In fact, it was the only "right" thing to do.

Love and justice should never be contrasted. Justice is itself possible only because of a prior love. Only love can guide power in the achievement of justice. Paul Tillich in *Love, Power and Justice* persuasively argues that in personal relationships there are three functions of the creative kind of justice: listening, giving, forgiving.

Paul's doctrine of justification by faith means precisely the acceptance of the guilty sinner (forgiveness of sin). To "justify" is to proclaim and make the sinner just. God does the right thing in making the unjust just, the unrighteous righteous. In short, the only road to justice is often the road of forgiveness, possible in Christian love.

The approach to justice which proceeds along the line of balancing the books is legalistic and impotent; the approach to justice which proceeds on the basis of recognizing and caring for persons means something quite different by the question, What is right? Among persons, forgiveness is often the only solution. And frequently it is the best solution. Forgiveness sets the person in a new relationship so that he can solve other problems.

God says to us when we question whether it is right to forgive, or whether the other person has adequately repented, "Forgiveness is just; you forgive. It is always right to forgive. Your forgiving will never undermine justice."

"Forgiveness Is Restoration"

We have previously noted that forgiveness of sins is reconciliation and that reconciliation is a restoration of personal relationship previously disrupted by sin. But, forgiveness is restoration in other ways which are often overlooked. Forgiveness is *healing* to those whose sins are as illness; forgiveness is *freedom* to those enslaved to sin; forgiveness is *cleansing* to those burdened with guilt; to the fallen forgiveness is *reinstatement.*

The psalmist described forgiveness of sin as a restoration to health. His "body wasted away" and his "strength was dried up as by the heat of summer" (Ps. 32). But forgiveness restored him to health and joy. In the New Testament, there is a clear relationship between forgiveness and healing. Jesus spoke to the paralytic, "My son, your sins are forgiven" (Mark 2:5), and later equated this statement with, "Rise, take up your pallet and walk" (Mark 2:9). After he had restored sight to the blind man at Jericho, Jesus said, "Your faith has made you well" (Luke 18:42). Forgiveness is related to healing in the Epistle of James (5:13–16).

Forgiveness is a glorious *healing.* The burden of sin does

result in a kind of illness which the psalmist so well described. We have all been ill from, or have seen others ill from, bearing grudges, unwilling to forgive and be forgiven. The only cure is forgiveness. We all know many individuals and groups desperately ill who can be healed only by forgiveness.

As liberation from bondage to sin, forgiveness is restoration to *freedom.* This is the theme of Psalm 51. The biblical words, "to send away," "to lift a burden," "to blot out," and "to deliver," dwell on the deliverance from sin. In biblical faith, life apart from God is life in bondage to sin. Forgiveness restores one to genuine freedom to be God's creature. One who has been forgiven is able to forgive others thereby freeing them from bondage so that they too can live in creative freedom.

When sin is seen in terms of stains, forgiveness is *cleansing,* a restoration to innocence. Isaiah (1:18–20) speaks of God calling his people to reason with him. Forgiveness will remove their blood-red stains; forgiveness will make them "white as snow" and "like wool."

To the fallen forgiveness is *reinstatement.* Forgiveness is incomplete so long as the guilty remains "outside." He must be restored. The symbols of restoration for the prodigal son were the robe, the ring, the shoes, and the banquet. The father ordered, "Bring quickly the best robe, and put it on him; and put a ring on his hand, and shoes on his feet; and bring the fatted calf and kill it, and let us eat and make merry; for this my son was dead, and is alive again; he was lost, and is found" (Luke 15:22–24).

Genuine forgiveness does not leave the forgiven as he is; it restores him to what he was or was intended. Forgiveness is not probation but restoration. A son must have the symbols marking full membership in the family: the robe, the ring, and the shoes. The feast celebrates the reunion of the family.

The apostle Paul counseled all churches when he advised the Corinthian church (2 Cor. 2:7) that their discipline of an erring member must culminate in forgiveness and reinstatement. He admonished them "to forgive and comfort him, or he may be overwhelmed by excessive sorrow." Reinstatement of the estranged is the goal of forgiveness. Hosea did not forgive Gomer *in absentia;* he went to the slave market and purchased her and took her back to the home (Hos. 3:2).

Offended Christians often deceive themselves into believing that they have forgiven the offender if they have reduced their ill will toward him from resentment to toleration. It is not forgiveness until the forgiven is reinstated, fully restored.

"Everyday Nonreligious Forgiveness"

In the previous paragraphs, we have dealt with the forgiveness of sins in the biblical or Christian sense. Most of what I have said has been somewhat "religious" as most people use the term. I have presupposed that my readers are either Christians or inclined toward Christianity. But I wish now to emphasize that most of us live most of our lives in a "nonreligious world" among "nonreligious" people who in our present decade favor the secularization even of the religious. What does our doctrine of forgiveness say about life in that setting?

Jesus told a little story in plain language about a good Samaritan who incidentally (as he journeyed) did a greater act in God's sight than either the priest or Levite who were professional religionists. The story which stands as a literary masterpiece of all time, points out that his unnamed traveler stopped to care for an unnamed victim of a mugging. In the story there are no details about the "religion" of the Samaritan. Apparently, Jesus meant to say that this man had done the will of God in his purely human act of caring for the wounded man. He recommended, "Go and do likewise" (Luke 10:29–37).

The Christian has a hundred opportunities to forgive and recommend forgiveness to every one opportunity to present his religious doctrine of forgiveness. We work among people who are inwardly torn because they don't know how to forgive themselves. We mingle with countless multitudes of estranged people who could be reconciled by the simple act of forgiving. We Christians can display a forgiving spirit and heal others by forgiving and by suggesting that they forgive one another. This incidental ministry may never issue in a "convert." In most instances, these people may never know our own "religious" stance; but, they can come to know some of the healing and reconciliation we have learned in Christ even if they are not disposed toward our religion or any religion.

The recommended incidental forgiveness is not the same as forgetting one's religious moorings. It is an expression of those moorings. But, it is a known fact that most of our opportunities to help people in the world fall outside of the religious lines which have been artificially drawn. So many of the problems of life have no solution except forgiveness. Many lives can be uplifted and liberated from needless burdens if a man of forgiving spirit can suggest or display forgiveness at the crucial time.

As "salt of the earth" and "light of the world" Christians should take their forgiveness into the secular world and share it without requiring religious prerequisites. They should forgive and demonstrate forgiveness in the purely secular areas of life. By so doing, they identify themselves with Jesus Christ and unconsciously witness for him.

"Forgiveness As Christian Witness"

The nonreligious ministry recommended previously may well lead to a discussion of and the full experience of Christian forgiveness. Practicing the art of forgiveness may well be one of the most effective approaches to Christian evangelism. The cheerful experience of the spirit of forgiveness may well open locked doors as people become interested in the "source" of this spirit.

Two passages come to mind. Jesus instructed, "If your

brother sins against you, go and tell him his fault, . . . you have gained your brother" (Matt. 18:15). Paul interpreted the Christian's task as a "ministry of reconciliation," and Christians as "ambassadors for Christ" with a "message of reconciliation" (2 Cor. 5:19–20).

In the first instance, we maintain relationships only by forgiveness, and the offended party must take the initiative. This requires a genuine spirit of love, and strength of character. The burden is on the stronger; the task is to reclaim the weaker. This is Christian. It is also an often-neglected form of ministry. Congregations are filled with people waiting for offenders to repent and come confessing before being forgiven. The Christian approach is to reclaim them by aggressively seeking them and forgiving them.

In the second instance, we go to the world as representatives of Christ the great reconciler who "gave his life a ransom for many." We go with a message that God will forgive; we practice a ministry of proclaiming forgiveness and of forgiving. A Christian cannot hope to win a lost person to Christ on any basis other than a full acceptance of him just as he is. Often, he is painfully aware of his numerous sins against God and men. The sinner's feeling of hopelessness stands between him and God's forgiveness. The Christian witness, by accepting him as he is, displays the spirit of Christ and introduces the lost man to God's forgiveness.

By presenting Christ's forgiveness, absorbing by love the sins of others, the Christian shows the estranged how to be reconciled to God.